LET'S TALK

LET'S TALK

Peer reviewed by Mayvrill Freeston-Roberts, BACP Accredited and Registered Counsellor and Psychotherapist

An Hachette UK Company
www.hachette.co.uk

Vie Books, an imprint of Summersdale Publishers Ltd
Part of Octopus Publishing Group Limited
Carmelite House
50 Victoria Embankment
LONDON
EC4Y 0DZ
UK

www.summersdale.com

Printed and bound in China

ISBN: 978-1-80007-175-9

Substantial discounts on bulk quantities of Summersdale books are available to corporations, professional associations and other organizations. For details contact general enquiries: telephone: +44 (0) 1243 771107 or email: enquiries@summersdale.com.

Disclaimer
Neither the author nor the publisher can be held responsible for any loss or claim arising out of the use, or misuse, of the suggestions made herein. None of the views or suggestions in this book are intended to replace medical opinion from a doctor. If you have concerns about your health or that of a child in your care, please seek professional advice.

LET'S TALK

A Boy's Guide to
MENTAL HEALTH

Adam Carpenter

CONTENTS

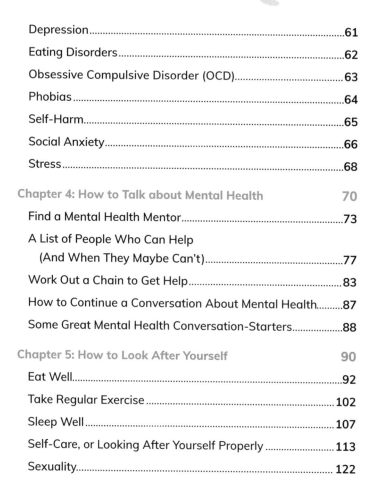

INTRODUCTION

Welcome to Let's Talk: A Boy's Guide to Mental Health.

Wait, what is mental health, exactly?

Ah, good question. Let's cut to the chase here. Mental health relates to how you are feeling mentally, i.e. what is going on in your mind. In the same way that your physical health relates to how you are feeling physically, in your body.

Examples of physical health issues are: a broken arm, a twisted ankle, catching a cold or the flu.

Examples of mental health issues are: depression, anxiety, stress.

Don't worry if some of these words are a little unfamiliar, because this book will help you understand the different types of mental health issues and offer advice on coping with any you may encounter.

Primarily, though, the aim of this book is to equip you with ways to make sure you stay in good mental health by talking openly about your feelings and being aware of your emotional needs. In your teens, if not before, you will likely face some difficult times – such as worrying about exams or school work, or maybe friendship or relationship problems – but you will get through them and the advice in this book will help.

"BUT I DON'T WANT TO TALK!"

I HEAR YOU SAY!

OK, let's address this title thing.

Talking DOESN'T have to involve talking to another person, although this will certainly be something that can really help people process any issues regarding mental health. First and foremost, the conversation you should be having is with...

YOURSELF!

Think of it like an inner voice you have before you take a test at school, play a football or basketball game or perform a song on your guitar.

Whatever it is, you mentally prepare by saying things like...

I **CAN** DO THIS!

WE **WILL** WIN THIS GAME!

Even reading this book is a form of conversation, and hopefully I will be able to share a lot of positive tips to help keep your mind and mental health in tip-top condition.

HOW TO USE THIS BOOK

I would recommend reading this book from beginning to end to gain a real understanding of your mental health and recognize when others might need support too. There's also cool stuff about how the brain works and ways to open a conversation around mental health if you do want to talk about it with someone else.

You will learn techniques and actionable tips to keep yourself in good mental health. These are skills that will help throughout your life, not just your teens.

The contents page will, of course, signpost you toward specific mental health conditions if you already know the one you want advice on.

And if you don't quite know what might be wrong, we have put together a simple quiz in Chapter 1 to pinpoint what support you (or someone you know) might need.

"NO, THAT'S IT – I'M OFF,"

This is something my teenage son might say.

But I think he would also be astute enough to hang on to a book like this. Not because it is written by his dad but more because he'd recognize that even though he might be feeling good in his mind one day, on another day he might feel sad, anxious or stressed.

What do you do when you don't feel very good in yourself? Who do you tell? How can you feel happy again?

The answer to all those questions begins with the very thing that you are holding in your hands. Clue: it isn't the Xbox controller, it's this book! And it's here whenever you feel you need some help or support.

TIP: GIVE YOUR MIND A BREAK FROM THE SCREEN

Fact: One in three internet users across the globe is UNDER 18!

I am hoping there will be nothing in this book that I mention or advise that I wouldn't do myself. To this end, I started writing the first draft by hand because I recognize how much easier it is to focus my mind away from all the alerts and notifications and temptations of going on YouTube that sitting at a computer or being on a smartphone or tablet can bring.

Even though I will have used Google to find out the above fact (thanks to the worldwide children's agency UNICEF), anything you can do to decrease your number of screen hours or minutes in a day will really help to keep your mind in good shape.

Another fact: Some research suggests screen time can have a negative impact on kids, while other research finds no evidence that it does.

So, don't worry about what the science says and instead listen to your own mind and body. If you are on a screen feeling groggy or lethargic, then step away from it. Go and read a comic or a book or go outside if you can. If you can't get outside, stand up and stretch, jiggle about, put your hands above your head and swoosh your arms down to your sides as if you are making a snow angel standing up! Any movement will help you take in some oxygen and even make you smile if you feel silly doing it.

Chapter 1

SO, WHAT'S THE PROBLEM?

Don't be afraid to ask for help when you need it... Asking for help isn't a sign of weakness, it's a sign of strength.

BARACK OBAMA

HORMONES

"Oh, it's not unusual to be down and moody in your teens. It's just your hormones."

This is most probably something you'll hear from people from time to time when you find yourself suddenly feeling low or angry for little or no reason at all. And it is, actually, true. As you go through puberty, you have this pea-sized blob at the base of your brain called the pituitary gland. This gland does indeed release hormones that can lead you to have sudden and intense mood swings for seemingly no reason at all. Your parent or carer could serve up your favourite meal for dinner and out of the blue, you might just feel angry at them for being nice. Or something like your friend cancelling a cinema trip with you could leave you feeling overwhelmingly sad, like it's the end of the world. Why is it doing this? Well, it's like the main gland that controls your metabolism, growth, sexual maturation and many other vital physical functions and processes so with so much for it to do, you'll forgive it for making you feel that way from time to time.

The good news is that these feelings are totally normal, they will pass and they're absolutely nothing to worry about.

The problem is when the low feelings stick around, because this might be depression rearing its ugly head. It is crucial that you don't listen to the "it's just your hormones" explanations during these times. This is where you need to remember the following...

TIP: IT'S OK NOT TO FEEL OK – YOU ARE NOT ALONE

Do not let anyone make light of your low or sad feelings with phrases like "you'll get over it" or "smile – crying won't make you feel better". This is actually known as TOXIC POSITIVITY where people believe that no matter how bad things are, you should maintain a positive mindset. Negative emotions aren't nice but they should not be ignored or brushed aside.

It really is OK not to feel OK.

More to the point, it is not YOUR problem to deal with alone. There is so much help out there, such as counsellors and school safeguarding staff. And, fortunately, this help is provided by people who are likely to have been through mental health issues that you might encounter in your own life. Their help, without a doubt, will make you feel better.

Whereas, left untreated and ignored, the problem will only get worse. It will not go away.

So, ignore toxic positivity and listen to people who say things like, "Things are tough for you right now, how can I support you?" Or "It's OK to feel this way. Do you want to talk about it?"

Of course, you might find it really hard to open up and talk to your parent, guardian or another caring adult, or maybe you have tried but they don't seem to get how you're feeling. If that is the case, can I just say...

PLEASE, PLEASE DON'T GIVE UP!

Here are some solutions to help you start those conversations, based on the barriers you may have already encountered:

BARRIER: "I find talking to my parents/teachers so cringe."

SOLUTION: Maybe start by talking about what you are going through in the third person – start everything you want to say with the phrase "I have a friend who..." This may make it easier for you to get your words out in the open and your chosen confidant will soon realize you are talking about yourself.

BARRIER: "My parents have problems of their own. I don't think they have the time to deal with mine."

SOLUTION: Your problems will likely be more important for them to solve than their own and helping you might be a welcome distraction and put their own difficulties into perspective. Pick a moment when your parents don't seem distracted by their problems, maybe when they are sitting down reading a book or newspaper.

BARRIER: "I've told my parents but they don't seem to understand."

SOLUTION: Have you seen anyone on YouTube or television or even in the news going through a similar problem that you are experiencing? Show your parents the YouTube clip or news article and say this is what you think you are going through. Hopefully it will help them understand and leave you feeling more comfortable talking to them about it.

If you are still finding it difficult, the ultimate BARRIER might be that you have chosen the wrong person to confide in. The SOLUTION is thinking of someone else who you feel more comfortable speaking to and who will listen and offer support. That person might be someone you don't know, such as a professional counsellor.

In Chapter 5, we will discuss all the people with whom you can talk about your mental health in more detail.

Just remember – and it is worth repeating – it is not just YOUR problem to deal with, you are not alone.

SO, WHAT IS THE PROBLEM?

You might be feeling irritable, argumentative or moody, or going through a period of anxiety, stress or low self-esteem. These are very common in people of all ages. When you are a teenager, these problems can seem magnified as it's a time of great change, both physically and emotionally, plus there is the added pressure of school and exams, and you're also figuring out who you are and what you want to be. That's a lot to deal with!

A lot of the time, low or angry feelings will soon pass. Some of the advice in this book will help you manage your stress and anxiety. Other times, you'll still find these feelings hard to shake, and that is when it is a good idea to open up to someone you trust who can direct you toward the support you need.

Of course, there are other, more serious, mental health problems which we will touch upon but the important thing to remember is that whatever the problem actually turns out to be, there is a way to deal with it that will make you feel better. All you need to do is take that first step of recognizing it and telling someone.

DON'T WORRY — YOU'VE GOT THIS!

QUIZ: HOW IS MY MENTAL HEALTH?

One way to determine whether you do need some mental health support is to answer the following five questions:

1 When you're feeling low, does doing something you enjoy make you feel better? YES/SOMETIMES/NO

2 Do you enjoy going out with your friends or spending quality time with your family? YES/SOMETIMES/NO

3 No matter how you feel, do you make sure you eat properly? YES/SOMETIMES/NO

4 Have you been sleeping well recently? YES/SOMETIMES/NO

5 At school, do you feel you have been doing your best work? YES/SOMETIMES/NO

If you have answered YES to three or more of the questions, then you are probably in good mental health – but wait! Don't put this book aside just yet as there's heaps of advice to help you stay that way.

If you have answered SOMETIMES to most or all of the questions, then don't worry – there is most likely some simple advice that you can follow to get yourself feeling better. All the questions are connected with positive ways to look after yourself so if you are not giving most of them your full attention a lot of the time, you could be in need of support to see what is at the root of your reluctance to do so. You are not being lazy or irresponsible. Something is driving you to feel this way and you may have an idea as to what it is. Check out Chapter 2 for some of the things that might be affecting you, such as pressure of exams or the recent loss of a loved one.

If you have answered NO to just one question, head to Chapter 5 and see if the advice given in the relevant section can nudge you into the "sometimes" or "yes" category for that question. If not, you will most likely require further support.

If you have answered NO to more than one question, you could be suffering from a mental health issue or condition. Head to Chapter 3 for an introduction to common mental health conditions, or look up in the contents if you already suspect what it might be.

This quiz, or indeed this whole book, is by no means going to lead you to a definitive diagnosis. Always see your doctor before you dive too deeply into thinking you have one particular issue, when it may be another. But this book should help point you in the right direction, give you an idea of what you might be experiencing and help you work out if you need further support.

WHAT HAPPENS WHEN YOU IGNORE YOUR MENTAL HEALTH?

N ow you may be thinking: OK, so I'm feeling a bit down or stressed – it will pass.

Sadness and stress are natural and do pass, it's if they don't that professional support should be sought.

To put it another way, if you are struggling with anxiety or depression, if left untreated, you may end up feeling physically unable to get up and go to school or walk into a classroom of people or plough through another English homework assignment.

Ultimately, no-one wants to end up lying on the sofa or in bed all the time because they mentally feel unable to do anything. Which is why looking after your mental health is so important.

WON'T MY MATES TEASE ME FOR TALKING ABOUT MY MENTAL HEALTH?

Sadly, even today, talking about "mental health" can come with a bit of stigma attached. In the school playground, some kids will show just how misinformed they are in terms of what mental health is and will be quick to dismiss other people who say they are feeling depressed or lacking in self-esteem.

Some will even accuse them of being "mental" – "yeah, he's mental, bro. Well mental, yeah – what a nutter!", etc.

Don't be one of those clowns – sorry, misinformed kids – for two main reasons:

1 The sooner you can equip yourself with information about looking after your mental health, the sooner it can make a positive difference, not just to your teenage years but for the rest of your life.

2 Someone with an issue such as depression needs your care and consideration as much as someone with a physical illness. You wouldn't mock or ignore someone in the playground with a broken leg. You would do your best to get them around the school, and find a way to help them. Imagine someone who says they're feeling low with a bandage around their head. It's not visible but it's there and they need people like you to be on the lookout for them – or at the very least to be considerate of their feelings.

SO, DO I HAVE A PROBLEM?

In all likelihood the answer to that question is no – see the quiz on page 20. The main purpose of this book is to increase your awareness of your mental health and help you feel comfortable talking about it so you can keep it in good shape – not just through your teens but, hopefully, for the rest of your life. Head over to Chapter 5 if you want to fast track to that bit.

If you have an idea as to what you might be going through, we'll be listing common mental health conditions in Chapter 3, together with ways to deal with them.

And in Chapters 4 and 6, we'll look at ways to start talking about mental health – both your own and also how to get other people to open up about theirs.

Finally, in Chapter 7, we will list some of the organizations that you can reach out to for support.

But first, let's delve into the idea of what "mental health" means for teenagers in particular in the context of the things that could be going on in your life, from exams to rocky relationships.

Just because you don't understand it, doesn't mean it isn't so.

TIP: IF THE TERM "MENTAL HEALTH" MAKES YOU CRINGE, DON'T USE IT!

How about starting a discussion about mental health without actually saying "mental health"?

The term "mental health" has done wonders to get people talking about the way they are feeling in their mind and emotionally. But, yes, the very words may make you cringe saying them in front of your mates.

When you think about it, we don't use the phrase "physical health" to talk about our physical health. Instead we target particular parts of the body... "my arm's playing up" or "I've got a sore foot."

So, if you are feeling a bit self-conscious using the term "mental health", DON'T USE IT!

The phrase "How are you feeling?" can be used to ascertain whether someone has a sore foot or a broken leg but usually it is meant more as a way to learn if a person is happy, sad, worried or stressed.

Remember: talking about mental health doesn't mean there is something wrong with you. It is a way to keep your mind healthy.

Chapter 2

WHAT'S HAPPENING TO ME?

IN YOUR MIND

As doctors are able to see what has happened to your body when something goes wrong, so too have psychologists study the mind and behaviour in order to understand mental health conditions. In this chapter we explore a little of the workings of the amazing organ that is YOUR teenage brain. You'll find techniques such as meditation to help manage these states of mind and again we will learn how the brain responds to these methods.

Of course, your mental health is very much affected by circumstances outside of your mind and body, and these circumstances could either be boosting your mental health or be draining it of its strength. We will look at some of the "drainers" such as peer pressure from your mates, stress from schoolwork and exams, or from family. Pressure is the key word here and we will suggest ways to keep it to a minimum.

Sorry, did I lose you at "meditation"? Please bear with me. The first part of this chapter especially is FASCINATING.

THE TEENAGE BRAIN

Brains are amazing. I mean, our bodies are incredible but the brain is the control centre to all the other parts. It controls our senses, our breathing, temperature and hunger – in fact every process that regulates and moves our body.

For instance, wiggle your toes.

Go on, do it.

Your brain just sent the message down the nerve cells in your spinal cord and told the muscles in your toes to wiggle them. Brilliant!

Not only does the brain control the body, it is also in the driving seat when it comes to the mind, controlling our thoughts, memory and emotions.

But wait – isn't "brain" just another word for "mind"? No, it isn't. Our brain is a tangible physical organ in our body. Our mind isn't – you can't point to a picture of the brain and go, that bit there is the mind. The mind is related to consciousness, the product of brain activity.

If doctors could fix the mind like they can fix a broken leg, then we might never get overwhelmed by bad mental health.

Instead outside forces, both good (e.g. having a laugh with a friend) and bad (e.g. finding out you have a maths test in the morning), instigate chemicals in the brain that affect your mind, i.e. how you feel.

THE GOOD BRAIN CHEMICALS

These are the chemicals in the brain that we need to kick in to ensure good mental well-being:

- **Dopamine – triggered by rewards or things you don't yet have. It's a great tool to motivate you to achieve things. Enjoy a boost of it by promising yourself a treat after doing an hour's solid revision.**
- **Serotonin – this can help you feel calm, confident and patient and can be triggered by sunlight.**
- **Oxytocin – aka "the cuddle hormone" is produced through social bonding. See the section about hugging on page 44.**
- **Endorphins – these are triggered by pain or stress and are released to reduce pain and boost pleasure. They can also be sparked by eating well and exercising.**

The mind is especially vulnerable when you are a teenager because the teenage brain has a lot of plasticity. It can change and adapt to its environment more easily than an adult brain. In some ways this is really good, for instance it is a great time to learn new skills and be creative.

Your prefrontal cortex isn't fully developed either. This is the brain's rational part and it means as a teenager, you are more likely to take risks rather than consider any long-term consequences. For instance, as a kid, I could jump into a swimming pool without a second thought. Now, though, I will hesitate and consider the implications if I hit the water in the wrong way.

Then there are your testosterone levels, that rocket during puberty. Testosterone is a sex hormone that influences your muscle mass, strength and gives you male characteristics such as facial hair and a deep voice. But the levels also affect your brain, again making you more likely to take risks and also liable to overreact in situations where you feel stressed, angry or hurt.

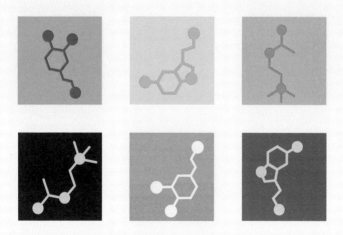

The brain is a
muscle that can
move the world.

STEPHEN KING, AUTHOR

TIP: USE 'EM OR LOSE 'EM!

During puberty the brain starts snipping away at the connections between its cells (aka neurons) that are not being used to make it more efficient as you go into adulthood. So if you started learning a musical instrument in primary school but gave it up, the brain will start to forget all that you learned unless you keep practising. I'm not saying that you cannot do so later in life but it will be more difficult and quite frankly, you will have less time to practise piano. Keeping these skills alive and at a level where you can do them with some finesse will provide you with an outlet where you can escape everyday stresses.

However, having such an adaptable brain also means it can be negatively affected by changes in your physical, social and emotional environment. In 2020 a Swedish study of teenagers over a period of five years discovered that family environment affected brain development more than genes. And research by the World Health Organization found that multiple physical, emotional and social changes, including exposure to poverty, abuse or violence, can make teenagers vulnerable to mental health problems.

Yet the good news is that the teenage brain is extremely resilient. In all likelihood you are on the path to becoming a perfectly healthy adult. Some of the changes happening in your brain may actually go on to protect you against mental health disorders. The trick is to learn how to keep those "drainers" at bay with "boosters".

DEVELOPING THE ART OF MINDCRAFT

Imagine your mental well-being is like a video game – or *Mindcraft!* – with the following levels:

Mentally THRIVING –
you feel you're doing
everything like a boss.

LEVEL 9 – 10

LEVEL 6 – 8

Mentally HEALTHY –
you feel happy
and valued.

Mentally LOW –
you feel sad.

LEVEL 3 – 5

LEVEL 1 – 2

Mentally UNWELL –
you feel really depressed.

The aim of the game is to keep your baseline above level 6. To achieve this, you must:

- **Gather the things that help promote good mental health – aka "boosters" – such as exercising or eating well.**
- **Avoid the things that cause bad mental health – aka "drainers" – to avoid pushing you below level 6, such as worries about schoolwork or mean friends.**
- **Deal effectively with "unavoidable events" like falling ill or a pet dying by employing the correct "boosters".**

We want to equip you with "boosters" to keep you mentally healthy, whilst arming you with tools to zap the "drainers" and deal with any unavoidable events.

Warning: Reaching Level 10 is great but the pressure to stay there is a "drainer" that could lead you to dip below Level 6. More on this later!

So, first of all, let's take a look at some of the "boosters" that will keep you at level 6 and above! Hopefully you will be there already but you can still benefit from knowing how to stay there and how to get back to the same place should you feel yourself dipping to level 5 or below.

THE BOOSTERS

1. POSITIVE THINKING

Positive thinking can really help rewire our brain for the better and, done regularly, will push our brains into creating new clusters of "positive thinking" cells so it becomes second nature – rather like practising a musical instrument! So, remember the following:

Fact 1: You are brilliant.

Fact 2: The possibilities ahead of you are amazing – you will be able to achieve so much in the years to come.

Fact 3: you probably need to remind yourself of facts 1 and 2 more often because chances are, you hardly ever do.

When something in our day goes wrong, we are all too quick to apportion blame to ourselves, e.g. "I'm such an idiot" or "I'll never do anything right" or "I'm terrible at doing this!". Now don't feel bad about this, grown-ups do this a lot too. There have been a fair few times writing this book where I've reached a tricky point and taken ages to get a few words down and I've thought "I'm terrible at doing this!"

But there are two things to note here:

1   Nothing good ever comes from negative thinking. Tell yourself you can't do something and guess what, you won't be able to do it. You are more likely to get frustrated at every attempt rather than building up the confidence to get the task done.

2   You wouldn't talk to your friends in the same way, you probably wouldn't even talk to your worst enemy in the same way. So why talk to yourself like that?

So stop with the negative talk and start being nicer to yourself. Facts 1 and 2 are just two of many more positive thoughts you can have. What are the others? Well, grab a bit of paper and start making a list so you can have them to hand when you need to remind yourself. Here are a few more:

Fact 4: I can always learn from mistakes, instead of dwelling on them. Tomorrow really is another day.

Fact 5: I am kind and kindness never goes unnoticed.

Fact 6: I have friends and family who love me.

Fact 7: Fact 6 is true, even when it doesn't feel like it.

I'll even leave space for you to write some more on the next page but on one condition... you promise me that you will recite a few of them to yourself EVERY SINGLE DAY! Even when you don't feel like doing so – in fact, especially when you don't feel like doing so. You might not be in the right headspace to believe the words but just saying them will help lift you out of that negative mindset.

TIP: START THE DAY ON A POSITIVE NOTE

There is a brilliant way to do this dreamt up by B. J. Fogg, the author of a great book called *Tiny Habits*. He gets out of bed and the first thing he says – out loud – is: "it's going to be a great day." Now to a teenager, this might sound incredibly naff and you don't have to do it in your bedroom, you can say it in the shower or as you are leaving for school. You can even just say it to yourself rather than out loud, so long as you do say it.

Don't force it, says B. J. – there will be some days that you know are going to be challenging and you may wish to change the wording slightly, for example: "something great is going to happen today."

Make this a tiny habit and it will have you believing that the day ahead is going to be great, which is a much better starting point than filling yourself with dread as though the end of the world is nigh!

TIP: TELL YOUR FRIENDS THEY'RE BRILLIANT TOO!

That might sound "a bit lame" but you don't have to do it in a cheesy way. Nor should you stop ribbing or dissing one another for a laugh. But when it occurs to you and you witness or hear of your friend doing something really well, and maybe they haven't got the credit they deserve, then tell them "that was really good" or "I'm really impressed with what you did". Or if they do something nice and thoughtful, say in your own way something like "you're a top dude" or "I'm lucky to have you as a mate". The point is, if you and your friends can be one another's cheerleaders, then it adds further reinforcement to those days when you need help with your positive thinking.

Confidence is
the foundation of
friendship. If we give
it, we will receive it.

HARRY E. HUMPHREY, ACTOR

TIP: SPEAK UP AND BE HEARD

Another fact for you: your opinion, thoughts and words matter and they deserve to be heard.

As a teenager, it's easy to assume that no-one is interested in what you've got to say. At home, your parent or carer or siblings may talk over you, at school your teacher might choose the other kids to speak. In most cases they probably don't mean to be dismissive or to ignore you – in fact, they are likely to be pleased to hear you speak up. So, speak up! Speak clearly and slowly so you can be understood and get across what you want to say. If you don't feel confident enough to speak up, hold up your hand or wave and get the person you want to address to stop and listen to you. Being able to do this is an important life skill. It's fine to be the quiet one and to mostly say nothing, as long as it is out of choice and you know you can create the platform to speak up and be heard when you want to be.

2. TIDY ROOM = TIDY MIND

You might not win any awards for having a tidy bedroom (but if you do keep your room tidy, you deserve one) and you probably get nagged to clean it up on a regular basis.

You shouldn't just do it to appease your parent or carer, though. Studies have shown that being surrounded by clutter can bring on anxiety and even make a person feel depressed. Whereas a tidy room can make us focus better and increase our productivity. It also makes us feel less irritated and distracted.

So why not try the following:

- If tidying your whole room seems an impossible task, start small – clear out your sock drawer or one shelf on your bookcase at a time.

- Keep your desk clear – tidy it after you have finished your homework so you are not faced with a mess when you next have some to do.

- Avoid dumping grounds. Don't use a desk, chair or, let's be honest, your floor as a place to leave things you can't be bothered to tidy away. Tidy things away straight away and if there isn't a place for them, make one.

- Leave your clothes for the next day out and put everything you need in your school bag to make the morning routine that bit smoother. This will really help you start your day feeling in control, particularly important if you have a stressful event like an exam or sports match.

3. BE A KIND PERSON

When you do something that makes you feel ashamed, it takes up a lot of headspace, right?

You may beat yourself up about it, but the reality is we all make mistakes. Sometimes we can't help putting our foot in it – we're only human!

Being a good person doesn't just mean not being a bad person – it means doing good deeds.

A good deed might be:

- **Picking up some litter you see in the park.**
- **Helping an old person off the bus with their shopping.**
- **Raising money for a charity.**
- **Visiting a relative in hospital.**

Doing good deeds will not only make you a good person but it will make you feel happier and better about yourself.

4. HAVE A CRY

When the subject of well-being comes up at school, some kids (and adults too!) will mock the very idea of being open about our feelings. They'll say things like: "Man up!" "Pull yourself together!"

And the big one: "crying is for wussies!"

Nonsense!

Because – breaking news – crying ISN'T for wussies. It is extremely good for you. Why? Well...

- It is a perfectly normal reaction to an upsetting situation.
- It's the body's way of helping you to relax and improve your mind.
- It releases chemicals called endorphins which help improve your mood.

In short, if you feel like crying, find somewhere private or be with a friend or relative you can trust and DO IT! You'll feel better instantly. Once you feel calmer, think about what made you cry. Sometimes this will be obvious: your hamster dying, a piano falling on your foot, etc. Other times you won't know immediately. Luckily, this is where this book comes in.

5. KEEP ON HUGGING

OK, I know your cringe alarm will have sounded enough to be heard in the next town but trust me on this one.

When you were little, you doubtless hugged your parents lots of times every day. Hugging makes you feel connected, loved, you did it without thinking. But the older you get, the less you might feel like hugging your relatives.

It needn't be like this. A good hug from someone in your family who you love and trust can boost your oxytocin and make you feel happy, which has got to be a good thing.

If no one human ticks the box, then hug the dog – or your teddy!

6. FIND YOUR FLOW

Flow is the state of mind where you become fully immersed in an activity that you enjoy, to the extent that you are not thinking of anything else.

You're in the zone, feeling energized and totally focused.

The psychologist Mihaly Csikszentmihalyi, who coined the term "flow" in 1975, once said, "the happiest people spend much time in a state of flow."

You might be thinking: "What was that dude TALKING ABOUT?" But you probably already do something that puts you in a state of flow without realizing it. Playing that tricky, involved video game – that's flow. Playing a musical instrument or practising a particular sport you enjoy. Again, both flow.

Flow is useful in times of stress, whether to calm you down after a stressful incident or as a break from studying for an exam. Ideally, it is a state you should try to get into every day so it never becomes associated in your mind with negative occasions.

TIP: KEEP CHALLENGING YOURSELF

The focus achieved by flow may start to wane if you don't push yourself in whatever activity it is that you are doing. Csikszentmihalyi says that you should keep on setting new, achievable goals that require a certain degree of effort and skill to obtain. Once you reach that goal, set another. Boredom and repetition are the enemies of flow – imagine playing the same piece on the piano over and over. This boredom will gradually spoil the enjoyment and snap you out of your state of flow. As will other distractions – if you are trying to create something, whether drawing a picture or writing a story, why not do so in silence. Find the quietest room in the house and resist the temptation to put on any music.

Listening to music that you love, incidentally, can also lead you to achieve a state of flow but you have to be doing nothing else but listening.

These "boosters" are there for the taking every single day to help keep our mental well-being in a good place and help you battle against the following "drainers" and "unavoidable events" that will add to the pressures of growing up.

So we say bring them on... well, sort of...

Even though you're growing up, you should never stop having fun.

NINA DOBREV, ACTRESS

THE DRAINERS

1. SCHOOL

Hopefully, school isn't always a bad thing but it is probably at the top of most teenagers' list of things that causes them stress and unhappiness! It could be an increase in the amount of homework or upcoming exams that you need to study for, perhaps there are people in your class who make you feel down or a teacher you dislike and the feeling is clearly mutual. You need to tackle these problems early so you're not overwhelmed by them.

Practical ways to deal with problems relating to school:

- Organize your time so you spread out the work you have to do, rather than putting it off until the last minute.
- Find a calming, positive space at school where you can be alone or just with the people you want to be with. It could be a corner of the sports field or a space indoors, such as the library, where you can sit and read or catch up with school work so you don't have as much to do at home.
- Promise yourself a little reward once you have finished the school day or finished your homework, whether that is winding down by watching more of your favourite series on Netflix or catching up with friends online.

You can't expect to like every classmate and every teacher at school. Do your best to ignore or play down any who annoy you and maybe find allies in your friends who feel the same about them so you can have a moan (without being mean – remember, always be kind because you never know why someone is behaving in a particular way).

Good boosters to use when school is getting you down: positive thinking, calming techniques, mindfulness, exercise

2. BULLIES AND MEAN "FRIENDS"

You know the sort of person who puts you down, mocks you incessantly – it's a fine line between a "friend" who does this and a bully.

Practical way to deal with this:

- Tell someone about the bullying – a parent, teacher, carer or another adult that you trust. You must never feel like you should tackle bullies alone. Also, block the bullies on social media.

- Find new friends. Joining a club at school that interests you is a great way to meet new people. Or perhaps consider messaging someone you know through school or a friendship group to find out if you have some common interests. Also sit next to someone different in class or on the school bus – they could be a future buddy.

- Remember: it isn't you, it is them. Keep telling yourself that, every time they attempt to bully you or be mean. The hardest thing to do is to ignore the mean people and the horrible things they say but it is really the most effective and powerful way to stop them. Bullies get bored when they don't think they are having an effect on someone.

Good boosters to use to cope with bullies: talking to someone you trust, positive thinking, exercise, imagining slapping them in the face with a wet fish (but don't actually do this)

3. TOO MUCH SOCIAL MEDIA

The initial buzz you can get through interacting with your friends on social media and enjoying short videos, memes and posts can quickly get addictive. Be aware that social media has been shown to put you at risk of some of the other things in this list of drainers, from pressure to live up to others' perfect online lives to the online trolls who can make your life even more of a misery than being bullied at school.

Practical ways to deal with this:

- Set a limit of, say, half an hour on social media and then go and do something else.
- Avoid anything online that makes you feel anxious or upset. Find the laughter instead!
- Do not engage with anyone you do not know online. Make sure all your accounts are set to private so you can choose who follows and messages you.

Good boosters to use: Find your flow – the best way to distract your mind. FaceTime a friend, or speak to them in real life.

TIP: STEP AWAY FROM THE SCREEN

Social media can be a minefield of people who like to show off what they have or exaggerate how happy they really are. If you begin to feel envious of other people's (fabricated) lives on Instagram or TikTok, come away from your device and appreciate what you do have in your own world. Think up, or even write down, a list of three things that you are grateful for. You don't have to share it so don't worry how sentimental or silly any of them may seem.

You could even start keeping a "gratitude journal" which is like a diary that you write in all the things that have made you feel happy or grateful each day. It helps focus your mind on positive things.

If I was writing an entry for the day that I am writing this, I would put:

1. My eight-month-old puppy bounded around the living room with a doormat in his mouth.

2. Received a nice text from my teenage daughter where she thanked me for the advent calendar that I had bought her.

3. Saw my friend Jason and we shared lots of laughs, including when he was shouting instructions from the next room about how to operate his coffee machine and I just couldn't do it. So we had a diet cola instead.

4. BEREAVEMENT

At some point in childhood, you are likely to suffer some sort of bereavement. Loss affects everybody differently and grief is not a clear-cut process. When you lose someone close to you, it's important to talk about your feelings and be really patient with yourself.

Also know that it is totally OK to have these feelings in relation to a family pet – often this will be your first true experience of losing somebody special in your life and don't let anyone take this loss anything less than seriously.

Practical ways to deal with this:

- Tell your parents or closest adult how you are feeling and they can help you to get help you need, which could mean speaking to a doctor or teacher. Your teacher or doctor will be able to recommend a bereavement counsellor who you will be able to talk to and share how you are feeling.
- Start a memory box or a photo album and fill it with memories of the loved one you have lost. You could do this with another family member or close friend who is feeling the same loss.
- Let the tears flow. Choose a private place or find someone you feel comfortable being sad in front of, and then just cry. You will feel better.

Good boosters to use: Find a flow, have a cry, keep on hugging

5. CRUSHES AND ROMANCE

Your teenage years are quite a ride as far as your hormones are concerned. Hormones are the chemicals that cause the physical growth and sexual development that will carry you into adulthood. Not only do they spark physical changes such as your voice getting deeper, your facial and other bodily hair to grow, they lead you to having crushes on and falling for all manner of people. It is a fun time, but it can also be frightening and confusing as you come to slowly work out who you are and who you fancy. In Chapter 5 we will discuss sexuality in more detail and the bumps in the road that come with discovering who you are. And then there are the ups and downs of falling in and out of love and having your heart broken.

Practical ways to deal with this:

- **Teenage love may seem trivial to some, but it is anything but. You are experiencing real feelings that deserve respect and care. If you cannot talk to anyone at home, consider speaking to a friend, or if heartbreak takes hold and makes you feel sad, there are helplines listed in Chapter 7.**

- **Write down your feelings. If you can, keep a diary where you can talk privately to yourself about who you like and why. If you are worried about anyone reading what you have written, just throw it away – the important part is getting it out of your head so you can think things through.**

- **Do not elevate your crush to godlike status. They're just a person so don't ignore them or run away if they try to speak to you. If you want to speak with them, start by messaging** them on a social media platform where you both might be in the same group chat – just keep the conversation casual and don't make it obvious that you like them.

- Speak to a trusted friend about what to do next. Maybe they can help engineer a day out with your crush as part of a group of friends where you may be able to spend more time talking to them one-to-one.

Good boosters to use when you're having love troubles: Positive thinking, have a cry, be a kind person

Chapter 3

SOME MENTAL HEALTH CONDITIONS YOU MAY HAVE HEARD ABOUT

In this chapter, we shall list the common mental health conditions that you may have heard other kids or adults talking about, either in real life or on television or social media. It is to help familiarize yourself with the correct information as to what they are rather than encouraging you to self-diagnose.

Mental health problems don't define who you are. They are something you experience. You walk in the rain and you feel the rain but, importantly, you are not the rain.

MATT HAIG, AUTHOR

ANXIETY DISORDERS

The definition of anxiety is a feeling of worry, nervousness or unease. In small doses these feelings are normal and can be very helpful; nerves spurring us on in a school football match for instance, or worry and unease alerting us to the dangers of walking into a field where a sign says, "beware of the bull" but you may not actually be able to see the bull yet.

In terms of anxiety being a mental health issue, you are suffering from an anxiety disorder if these feelings of worry, nervousness or unease are ongoing, intense and out of control. So those nerves stop you from being able to move or do very much on the football pitch, or your worry and unease about bulls in fields make you feel panicked every time you have to walk through any field.

Early warning signs of suffering from an anxiety disorder include dizziness, shortness of breath, nausea and sleeplessness. It is important to take notice of these and address your anxiety with the help of a parent, teacher or friend who you trust. Otherwise, long-term effects of anxiety include withdrawing from family and friends, feeling unable to go to school and other places in a bid to avoid your fears.

TIP: FOUR SUPER-QUICK WAYS TO HELP MANAGE ANXIETY

Take slow, deep breaths – this will relax your phrenic nerve that runs from your diaphragm to your brain, and send a message to the entire body to loosen up.

Do ten push-ups – it sounds mad but any exercise sends oxygen to every cell in your body, so your brain and body operate at their very best. Go for a run or a kick about in the garden or school playground if you have time.

Think of a favourite memory – anything that will make you smile and focus on something good in your world is great ammunition against your sources of worry.

Focus on one of your senses – find a soothing smell or a calming sound outside, close your eyes and focus on it for a few minutes. It might sound silly, but it will help lower your heart rate and stop your mind from getting in a twist about whatever it is making you anxious.

BIPOLAR DISORDER

A form of depression where the sufferer goes from extreme highs to periods of feeling extremely low. The sufferer can experience these swings of mood over short or long periods – they could be full of energy and enthusiasm for a time and then switch to having feelings of emptiness, guilt or despair.

During a manic episode, a person will be more active than usual and say that they are extremely happy or high on life. They may also be quite impulsive during these periods.

During a depressive episode, they will be less active than usual and show little or no interest in things that normally excite them. Between these stages, the person will return to their typical mood.

Generally, bipolar disorder develops in your late teens or young adulthood but cases in younger people are not uncommon. There is no cure for bipolar disorder, but people can manage the condition with a range of treatments, including therapy and medication.

See also Depression on the next page.

DEPRESSION

P erhaps one of the most misused statements in the world is "I'm depressed" when really the person means "I'm sad". Sadness may feel overwhelming but through it, there will be moments where you are able to laugh and be comforted.

Depression, on the other hand, is a longer term mental illness. Sufferers will be unable to find enjoyment in anything, including activities and the company of people they used to enjoy. This doesn't mean they are constantly miserable as they will have coping mechanisms to cover up their condition. But all too often they will be unable to bring themselves out of their depressive state.

Other symptoms of depression include extremities such as eating too much or too little, sleeping too much or too little, extreme feelings of guilt or worthlessness.

Depression in young people is by no means rare and it is likely that one or more of a range of outside forces causes it, from a trauma early in life to a family history of mental illness, or lack of family or community acceptance about one's sexuality.

If you think you might be suffering from depression, see Chapter 7 (page 138) for ways to get help.

EATING DISORDERS

Though more prevalent in teenage girls, boys can also develop eating disorders, whether it is an obsessive compulsion to lose weight by undereating (anorexia) or binge eating and then vomiting (bulimia).

BEAT, the leading eating disorder charity in the UK, states that up to a quarter of sufferers can be men and that the kinds of stresses and worries that might lead to developing an eating disorder – such as work or academic stress, bereavement, relationship problems and struggles with body image – are not unique to one gender.

If you feel you might be becoming obsessed with losing weight or overexercising, speak to a trusted adult, someone who knows you and may have spotted a difference in you. They can guide you toward getting further help from your GP or an organization such as BEAT. As it states on BEAT's website, you can get treatment for an eating disorder and full recovery is possible. Contact details can be found in Chapter 7.

OBSESSIVE COMPULSIVE DISORDER (OCD)

A condition where a person experiences obsessive thoughts and compulsive behaviours. OCD is common in all genders and symptoms usually begin during puberty and teenage years. These symptoms can include repetitive behaviours to relieve anxiety or an obsessive thought or worry; for example, a fear of germs can lead to repeatedly hand-washing or cleaning.

OCD sufferers can feel embarrassed by their compulsions and reluctant to seek help, but it's important to remind the sufferer that it's not something to be ashamed of and there are psychological therapies available and support that they can access through their doctor.

PHOBIAS

A phobia is more than just being afraid of something. It is a type of anxiety disorder that will cause a person to feel anxious just thinking about or talking about their fear. A phobia can have a real impact on sufferers' day-to-day lives, causing them to make decisions based on avoiding their fears.

The good news is that counselling and therapy can help people deal with and manage a phobia. If you think your fear is affecting your life, then it is worth speaking to your doctor. Don't be embarrassed, whatever it is – there is pretty much a name for a phobia of anything.

SELF-HARM

Self-harm is the deliberate injury to oneself and usually it is associated with the manifestation of a psychiatric disorder. If this is something you are affected by, then really do take the first step to tell someone in your family or contact the Young Minds or Childline helplines in complete confidence. They will guide you toward getting help, their contact details are on page 147.

It is worth bearing in mind that an act of self-harm doesn't just mean that you cut yourself deliberately. If you have ever deliberately punched a wall, slapped yourself repeatedly in the head, bitten your hand in anger or anything like that, then that is a form of self-harm. Hopefully these are things you've done once, realized they hurt and then you have refrained from doing them again. However, if they are behaviours you return to on a regular, or semi-regular basis, you need to ask yourself why they are happening and seek help if you are unable to stop. Your doctor or school should be able to refer you to a counsellor.

SOCIAL ANXIETY

It is perfectly normal to feel "butterflies in your stomach" when faced with certain social situations, such as going on a first date or having to speak in front of the whole class.

But a person with a social anxiety disorder is likely to feel anxious about simple, every day interactions such as having to speak to a teacher or interact with other kids at break times.

The anxiety is fuelled by feelings of awkwardness and embarrassment, as though they are going to be continually judged and mocked by those around them. People might tell you this is not the case, but it won't stop you feeling like this and the fear and anxiety could lead to them avoiding all manner of social situations throughout your life.

Physical symptoms include: blushing, increased heartbeat, nausea, trembling, sweating and trouble catching your breath. In other words, way more than just "butterflies in your stomach".

If this sounds like you, it is best to seek help sooner rather than later. Sometimes social anxiety can be learned behaviour, such as from a parent or because of something upsetting that happened to you when you were younger. A doctor will be able to refer you to a counsellor.

TIP: WAYS TO EASE SOCIAL ANXIETY

- **Breathe slowly and deeply** (see Anxiety Disorders, page 58).
- **Focus on what people *are* saying**, not what you *think* they are saying.
- **Break down challenging situations into small chunks** – how, for instance, you might deal with each different encounter at a party, from thinking up an icebreaker to chat with someone you don't know, to how you'll manage to fill your plate at the food table without thinking everyone is watching and waiting for you to spill something.

STRESS

This is common in teenagers which is no surprise given the list of causes:

- **Schoolwork, homework, exams and pressure to do well.**
- **Relationships with friends, boyfriends and girlfriends.**
- **Feeling unprepared or overwhelmed by tasks.**
- **Family fights and break-ups.**
- **Big decisions, such as choosing subject options, deciding whether to leave a school club or break off a relationship with someone.**

It's stressful just looking at that list! But it really is important to realize when stress is taking hold and stopping you from dealing or coping with a certain situation in your life.

Symptoms include: moodiness and the sudden urge to cry, finding it hard to relax, nausea, loss of appetite, dizziness or unexplained pins and needles.

The expression "a problem shared is a problem halved" sounds twee but it can really work. Opening up to a parent or sibling, or a trusted teacher, relative or friend will get your troubles off your chest, and they are likely to help you find solutions and coping mechanisms that will reduce the stressful feelings. Making that first move sounds scary, I know, but stay tuned – we will talk about how to open up to someone in the next chapter.

TIP: TALK TO A CLOSE FRIEND

Why not consider speaking to a close friend about your stresses? It's possible they could be suffering from stress too and together you can form a stress-busting network, where you arrange to do something relaxing and fun that will help you put all your worries to one side. Alternatively, you could arrange to study for an exam or do some homework together, so you can tackle the school subjects you struggle with and help one another solve problems.

Chapter 4

HOW TO TALK ABOUT MENTAL HEALTH

In the previous chapter, we mentioned a fair number of mental health conditions that can begin to be addressed and managed by talking to someone. That someone could be a parent, sibling or another relative, a trusted teacher or even your doctor or a counsellor.

Talking to someone is a really important way to help look after your mental health, especially if you feel you are experiencing one of the conditions listed in the previous chapter.

You can live well with a mental health condition, as long as you open up to somebody about it, because it's really important you share your experience with people so that you can get the help that you need.

DEMI LOVATO, SINGER AND ACTOR

FIND A MENTAL HEALTH MENTOR

Why is talking to someone important?
Because the thought of having a mental health issue can be scary, so open up to someone close to you and they will:

- help you gain perspective on your situation.
- ensure you seek further help such as from a doctor or counsellor so you can get to the root of the problem.
- keep you positive by focusing on a brighter future.
- make sure you are not alone.
- if they see you struggling, they can help you with simple calming techniques such as breathing and mindfulness.

Please know that you can find the right person to confide in, even if you are reading this and thinking that isn't possible.

Don't worry, though. I am not expecting you to pick someone to open up to and then just let you get on with it. The aim of this chapter is to get you used to the idea of opening up about your mental health and helping you find the right person to speak to. We will discuss ways to broach the subject and overcome any awkwardness.

Remember, talking about mental health doesn't have to be scary. It is a step-by-step process and the first step involves opening up to the most important person of all, the one person you may not have thought about opening up to...

YOURSELF!

If you are reading this and thinking that you have never experienced any struggles with your mental health, well firstly, congratulations on getting this far into the book!

Secondly, and more seriously, can you honestly say that you haven't? Be honest. Think of the last time you had to study for a test at school or give a talk in front of the whole class. How stressed did you feel?

What about the last time you maybe had to go to a party or hang out with some people, some of whom you didn't know. How anxious did you feel?

Now the purpose of asking you these questions isn't so you suddenly go, "oh yeah I'm prone to stress" or "oh yeah, I suffer from a social anxiety disorder" because as we have seen in the previous chapter, the occasional incidences of these where the stressful and anxious feelings pass are perfectly normal. The point being is that did you recognize and acknowledge these at the time?

If you did, then you are aware of the times when you might find yourself hindered by your mental health and are more likely to spot it happening the next time.

If you didn't, hopefully these questions have made you aware when you are being hampered by your mental health in future.

For instance, the next time you are revising and suddenly feel overwhelmed with it all, you can tell yourself: "I am feeling stressed but I know I can do something about it and overcome it." You can consult a book like this or, better still, go and speak to someone, either a grown-up or a friendly classmate who is also having to study and maybe going through a similar experience.

Similarly, next time you feel nervous about being in a roomful of strangers, tell yourself: "I am feeling socially anxious but I know I can do something about it and overcome it."

In other words, acknowledging these feelings is a great first step but it is just a first step. And the crucial thing in both these examples is knowing when you need to reach out to someone. That's when you need to ask yourself: "OK, who can I tell about this?"

Which is a good question... who should you tell? And how do you go about telling them and asking for help?

Hopefully now you are not cringing but thinking that talking to someone is the right way to make your mind feel better again, just like when you fell over as a little kid and your mum or dad cleaned you up and gave you a plaster and a cuddle to feel better.

Let's find the right person to give your mind that plaster...

A LIST OF PEOPLE WHO CAN HELP (AND WHEN THEY MAYBE CAN'T)

So here they are, your potential mental health mentors in, it should be stressed, no particular order. Sometimes they'll be perfect in certain situations, less so in others...

PARENTS/GUARDIANS

If your immediate response is, "oh I could never talk to my parents about anything", I totally get that and they don't have to be your first port of call, even though they are likely to be the most accessible. There could be any number of reasons not to speak to them including, but not limited to:

- **They could have mental health issues of their own.**
- **They could be the reason for your stress or anxiety, e.g. if they are constantly putting you under pressure to do well at school.**

At some point, though, they will need to know about what you are going through so it's worth checking out page 83 to learn about working out a chain to get help, in order to reach out to them indirectly. You don't have to do this straight away. And do not feel you are betraying your parent or carer by not wanting to approach them in the first instance. You are the most important person here so if talking to someone other than a parent suits you better, then find that person.

I've not really sold you on talking to parents so far, have I? Hopefully your response will have been something along the lines of: "hmmm, well maybe I could speak to them first."

So do it. Pluck up the courage and do it. It's the job of a good parent to listen and understand and find ways to help you. You will feel better getting it out in the open.

Best for asking about: Issues they may have spotted you are going through; issues that may have been set off by a particular incident at home such as a big argument that became heated due to your stress or anxiety; anything related to something that one or both of your parents may have suffered with, such as depression.

TEACHER

There are two types of teacher you could speak to about a mental health issue: a trusted teacher or a teacher who has been given a title along the lines of Mental Health Champion. These are teachers who have been specifically trained in the subject of mental health and how to talk to students about such issues. Ask your school secretary who the teacher in question is, or consult your school handbook or website.

Not every school will have such a scheme and it might be a good opportunity to approach your head of year or even head teacher to see if there is something they can do to provide this very important resource.

Your trusted teacher could be your form tutor or one who perhaps teaches you and knows you well enough that you will feel at ease speaking to them.

Best for asking about: School-related stress and anxiety, but they should also be able to help or signpost you toward further support regarding any mental health condition you might wish to approach them about.

OLDER BROTHER OR SISTER

They may be an idiot/annoying BUT they are your sibling and, keep it quiet, they love you. They will be the first person to stick up for you in lots more circumstances than you know and they will likely have your back here if you can articulate how much a particular mental health issue is bothering you.

Best for talking about: Things you know they will have gone through, e.g. exam stresses or concerns you have about your parents or guardians.

FRIENDS

If you have already taken on board the advice about friends in Chapter 2, you might have a choice of a few to open up to. Pick someone who you feel certain will always have your back, and maybe is someone in whom you've confided before (or who has confided in you!)

Find a quiet moment to speak to them where you won't be disturbed and in the unlikely event that they turn out not to be the friend you have built them up to be, just backtrack and change the subject and make sure you find someone else to talk to instead.

Ask for clear advice and opinions on the situation but remember they are only about your age. They might not always have the answers or even the means to lead you toward further support. Great if they do, of course, but you don't want to make them feel as though they have the full responsibility of looking after you.

Best for talking about: School-related issues such as homework or exam stress. Issues that arise from the way other friends treat or talk to you.

OTHER RELATIVES

A trusted relative such as a grandparent, an aunt or uncle, or even older cousin might be the perfect compromise between speaking to someone very close to you like a parent or sibling, and someone who is that bit more detached from you like a teacher or friend. If you tell them you have something you wish to share in confidence, they should get the severity of the issue you are about to tell them about and offer assurance that they won't tell anyone else in the family until you are ready.

Best for talking about: Things you know they might have gone through and behaviours they may have seen when you were stressed or feeling depressed.

HELPLINES

If none of the above appeal to you then there are helplines out there where you can remain completely anonymous, with no-one judging you in any way.

A good starting point are Young Minds, Childline or Befrienders Worldwide, all of whom have trained counsellors who can simply listen to you share your troubles and guide you toward further help, and again this could simply be another helpline where your anonymity is guaranteed.

Search online for other, more specific organizations, you'll also find more information in Chapter 7.

Best for talking about: Anything! Just do that internet search!

If the thought of even speaking to someone you don't know fills you with dread, you will be pleased to know that a lot of the helpline websites have online chat and even text facilities. You can share your troubles as though you are writing them down for yourself, except you will get helpful encouragement and advice sent back to you.

WORK OUT A CHAIN TO GET HELP

You don't have to choose just one person to confide in about your mental health issue. If you have spoken to your parents, they are sure to be willing to speak to a teacher on your behalf to get further support, especially if it is something that might be affecting your schoolwork. Or, they could accompany you to the doctor to discuss further treatment, whether that is counselling, medication or a combination of both.

Your chosen parent, sibling or friend may have been a good listener but may require support themselves in order to help you further. If you have spoken to your sibling first, maybe they could help you to open up to one of your parents. Similarly, the right friend could pave the way in connecting with the best teacher to help, or even offer up good reasons and ways for you to tell your parents. Alternatively, you might just wish to open up to a friend to get a different perspective which may provide further comfort to you.

If you've shared with a trusted teacher first, they could broach what you feel is a tricky subject to your parents and provide a safe space where you can all discuss the problem further and what can be done to support you.

These combinations of people are like CHAINS toward getting the right help.

So what might your chain look like?

In order to work out a chain to get the help you need, divide a sheet of paper into three columns.

In the left hand column, list all the people you feel comfortable about speaking to in the first instance. In the far right column, list the people you feel that you need to open up to in order to access further help or support. You might be able to connect one person in the left column with the appropriate one in the right – if you cannot do this directly, use the middle column to add in people who will help connect them. If you would like to see a doctor but can't tell your parents directly, speak to your sibling and then they can tell your parents who can then help you get an appointment with the doctor.

WHO I FEEL COMFORTABLE SPEAKING TO	POSSIBLE CONNECTOR	WHO I NEED TO SPEAK TO

TIP: DON'T GIVE UP OPENING UP!

If the first person you choose to speak to about your mental health doesn't seem interested or isn't able to help you find further support, find someone else to speak to. Go to the next person on your list. Remember this...

YOU DESERVE HELP AND SUPPORT!

The reaction of the person who hasn't helped is about them, it's not you. Please don't let them stop you from reaching out again. There really is someone out there who wants to help you. Let me just say that again...

YOU DESERVE HELP AND SUPPORT!

HOW TO CONTINUE A CONVERSATION ABOUT MENTAL HEALTH

Well-being specialist Jonathan Phelan identifies three things to discuss when opening up about your mental health, specifically referring to conditions such as post-traumatic stress disorder:

1 Triggers – rather than focusing on your condition or issue, focus on the triggers that make you feel worse. What, in particular, can make you have a bad day? What makes you anxious or stressed? Your confidant may be able to help you avoid these triggers.

2 Resilient resources – these are things that make you feel better, so they may go back to finding your flow as in Chapter 2 (see page 27). Perhaps a certain style of music can keep you calm while revising.

3 Talents and abilities – we have a tendency to feel that a mental health problem takes over our whole life and nothing positive can be gained. Yet, people who struggle with their mental wellness can often be more creative, display strong logical thinking and judgement and have an increased empathy with other people.

SOME GREAT MENTAL HEALTH CONVERSATION-STARTERS

Before reaching out to someone for help and support, think of how you are going to broach the subject. Here are five mental health icebreakers, with space for you to jot down your own...

1   "You remember the other day when I..." – recall a shared experience where you felt your mental health issue was taking over.

2   "Did you see that episode of that show where the character..." – create a context by referencing something on television that your confidant may have seen and can relate to.

3   "I think I might be dealing with what that sports star had..." – someone famous may have raised awareness of your mental health issue in the news and this might resonate with the person you're speaking to.

4   "I don't think I am going to be able to do..." – if your mental health issue is preventing you from progressing with a particular school assignment or doing well in a school sport, work backward. Say what you don't think you will be able to do because of the issue, and let your confidante lead you to a different way of thinking so that you might just be able to do it after all.

5   "I'm not in a good place..." – honest and to the point – if you think your confidant can handle it, just get straight into it.

Add your conversation starters here...

Chapter 5

HOW TO LOOK AFTER YOURSELF

There are three main ways to help keep your mind in tip-top working order:

1 **Eat well**

2 **Exercise**

3 **Sleep well**

And eat well, did I mention eat well? Eating well is very, very, VERY important.

Anyway, this next chapter will focus very much on those big three, with time at the end to consider other good ways to look after your mental health.

EAT WELL

> **Good nutrition creates health in all areas of our existence. All parts are interconnected.**
>
> **T. COLIN CAMPBELL, BIOCHEMIST
> (AGE AT TIME OF WRITING: 87)**

Just as eating the wrong things can impact your physical health, so too can it affect your mental health. There is a strong relationship between our gut health and mental health – in fact our gut is often said to be our "second brain" – so when we eat healthy things like lean meat and fish, fruit and vegetables, it can really have a positive effect on our mood and well-being.

Whereas too much sugar, for instance, can trigger an imbalance of certain chemicals in our brain and make us more prone to depression. Eating too much saturated fat, meanwhile, will stop the body converting other food into the nutrients that the brain needs. Saturated fat is an unhealthy fat that is found in high amounts in butter, lard, cheese, sausages, bacon, chocolate, pastries, ice cream, cakes and biscuits. The trick is to have a little of these foods and make sure that you are mainly eating healthy food.

In short, eating healthily will make you feel well and perform better. Fact. Not only can having the good fats and/or protein found in foods like lean meat, fish such as tuna and salmon, leafy green vegetables, nuts and eggs be really good for building up your strength physically, do not underestimate the amazing connection between the brain and the gut.

Our guts and brain are linked via the vagus nerve, enabling them to send messages to one another. The gut can influence emotional behaviour in the brain, i.e. make you feel good or not so good, whilst your super clever brain can change the type of bacteria living in the gut for the better or the worse, depending on what you feed it! Lean protein found in chicken, fish and nuts can give it more energy to help it think and react quickly. It's also true that the more variety of healthy food you try and then incorporate into your diet, the more your brain will be kept happy and less prone to stress.

Half the battle of eating well is making sure you have the healthy foods and snacks that you like readily available and getting into the habit of loading up your plate with them. Check out some of the Challenges on page 97 to set you on the right path.

Now, I'm not saying that you should banish all sugary foods. They are there to be enjoyed... sometimes. Just don't make these things part of your regular, daily diet.

> **Eating healthy food fills your body with energy and nutrients. Imagine your cells smiling back at you and saying: "thank you!"**
>
> **KAREN SALMANSOHN. SELF-HELP AUTHOR**

If it came from
a plant, eat it.
If it was made in
a plant, don't.

MICHAEL POLLAN,
SCIENCE JOURNALIST AND AUTHOR OF
THIS IS YOUR MIND ON PLANTS

TIP: GET YOUR PARENTS INVOLVED

Your folks are the ones likely to be buying and cooking your food so you'll need to approach them about making changes and maybe they can do it too. A good way is for you all to fill in food diaries for a week, then go from there as to how you can make your diets the best they can be for body and mind.

"Mum, Dad... I want to eat more healthily..." shouldn't be a taboo conversation on either side.

AND REMEMBER... YOU ARE NEVER TOO YOUNG TO START EATING HEALTHILY

If you are in a family where junk food and ready meals are the norm, you could change everyone's lives in your household for the better. When my son, aged 11, decided he wanted a healthier diet, his cutting out sweets, chocolate and crisps had such a positive effect on the rest of the family. His mum was inspired to change the way she ate so she could form more healthy, sustainable eating habits, instead of resorting to fad "diets" from time to time. I found myself eating less sugary foods, not because I had an issue with my weight but because I realized alternatives were better for me and just as tasty. Even his big sister started monitoring the sweets she was eating, having just a few at a time instead of munching her way through whole bags which is easily done when you're a kid. His mum and me ended up exercising on a regular basis and this kept the healthier eating on track too.

So to reiterate, no-one is expecting you to ditch all the bad stuff overnight. Instead, why not pick just one or two things listed opposite over the next few weeks or months and see what difference they make to your well-being? You can track your progress by filling in the Food and Mood chart on page 101. Or, if you are not convinced that you could improve what you eat, why not start by filling in a simple food diary, logging what you eat in any one week.

In other words, forget trying to eat three cream crackers in a minute without drinking, if you are going to embark on a challenge like a YouTube content creator, why not break the mould and choose something that is good for you to do – and could well change your life for the better. Presenting the...

NO-SUGAR-FOR-A-WEEK CHALLENGE

No sugar for a week! Sounds like hell. But wait – think of diet drinks, they're pretty tasty, right? So why not try to substitute other sugary foods in the same way? You can get a lot of sugar-free treats from your average supermarket or pound shop. Here are some ideas:

- **Sugar-free cookies. I'm having one now, actually. They tick the biscuit box for sure. Do not knock 'em until you've tried them – the same goes for sugar-free chocolate chip cookies.**

- **Swap milk chocolate for high cocoa content dark chocolate. It will taste bitter and grainy to begin with but keep trying some each day until you have finished a whole bar (a couple of pieces a day is more than enough).**

- **Try baking cakes or cookies but swap the sugar for powdered sweetener like Stevia or Erythritol. There are lots of great sugar-free recipes online.**

- **"No sugar" means no refined sugars. It's fine to have natural sugars. So stock up on fruit such as apples and strawberries so you've plenty of healthy treats to banish any sugar cravings.**

- **Get the whole family involved. Can you all go without sugar for a week? Will your sibling be able to tell the difference between their usual sweet treat and a sugar-free variety?**

- **Record how you feel afterwards when you return to eating sugar again. Does it taste the same as before? How does it make you feel? You could even turn this into a great project for school by using the Food and Mood chart (see page 101) and win a few brownie points from your cookery teacher. Sugar-free ones, obviously.**

But wait, I hear you cry – sweeteners are worse for you than sugar, aren't they? They cause cancer. Actually, that is very much a myth – both Cancer Research UK and the US National Cancer Institute have confirmed they do NOT cause cancer.

All sweeteners have to undergo rigorous safety checks before they are allowed to be sold in our stores. I've mentioned Erythritol and Stevia as both are 100 per cent natural and can be used in combination in recipes (Stevia is sweeter whilst Erythritol has no aftertaste).

That said, as sugar-free products will always state, some sweeteners when eaten in great quantities can act as a laxative and make you go to the toilet a lot.

Make Water Your No.1 Lest we forget the importance of water in your diet. You don't actually need to drink litres of the stuff every day as we get a lot of the water we need from the food we eat. This challenge is more about making water your go-to drink of choice when you are thirsty. Bypass the sugary or even diet drinks for a week and choose water instead. See how it makes you feel.

OTHER FOOD CHALLENGES YOU COULD TRY

Have a Super Food Every Day. Here, in no particular order, are seven super foods you need to have in your life because they can give your mental health a boost (which is what makes them super):

- Fatty fish such as salmon or tuna – these contain plenty of omega-3s.

- Probiotic yoghurt – these contain live bacteria (not as gross as it sounds) to help improve your gut health.

- Bananas – high in vitamin B6 and prebiotic fibre which combine to keep your blood sugar levels stable.

- Blueberries – bursting with antioxidants and vitamin C that have been proven to lower anxiety and stress.

- Oats – yep, ditch the sugary cereal at breakfast and try oats in milk, heated up in the microwave with a swirl of honey on top. Yum!

- Avocado – green and slimy, yes and a potential hazard when cutting open (so scoop out the flesh and the stone with a spoon, NOT a knife), but lots more of that really good vitamin B6.

- Lentil soup – the key ingredient here is lentils, home to a fair bit of vitamin B that improves your mood by increasing your levels of chemicals such as serotonin and dopamine. Add in some healthy veg for more flavour and goodness.

TIP: DON'T GIVE IN TO PEER PRESSURE

Of course, it's fine to go out with your mates and enjoy a burger and chips or pizza and ice cream, but make sure it is your choice to have these foods. If part of you wishes to pick something healthier from the menu, then do it. Don't be worried about what your friends might say. Chances are they won't even notice or, more likely, they will see you setting a good example to break from the norm and have something that is good for you. If any one of them starts mocking you for your healthy option, then you have to wonder if they are a true friend.

FOOD AND MOOD CHART

It looks like homework but it isn't homework – it is the key to seeing just how much food can change the way you feel – for better or for worse.

DATE & TIME	HOW GOOD I FEEL BEFORE EATING (out of 10)	WHAT I ATE	HOW GOOD I FEEL STRAIGHT AFTER EATING (out of 10)	HOW GOOD I FEEL 30-60 MINS AFTER EATING (out of 10)

It is important to fill in the second column before eating what you are about to eat, if you can. Equally, the two after eating numbers will give an indication of how the immediate fix of having eating something compares with how you feel a short time afterwards. Of course you are going to feel good immediately after eating a tasty doughnut – but how will you feel half an hour later?

Don't waste your time by making up numbers or leaving funny comments like "I still feel hungry" in column four – give some thought to the mood you are in.

TAKE REGULAR EXERCISE

According to a study by the World Health Organization in 2018, over 80 per cent of schoolkids across the globe aren't getting the recommended one hour of physical activity a day.

I hear ya... one hour... a day? I'm not even doing one hour a week.

Well, it's time to change that – not just for the sake of your long-term physical health but also for your mental health. In fact, if you exercise, you are much more likely to see an immediate impact on your mental health.

Why is exercise so good for your mental health? Because it releases so many good chemicals in your body, such as endorphins that make you feel happy, and norepinephrine that calms the brain's response to stress and anxiety.

In a nutshell, exercise can:

Your self-esteem
Your confidence
Your energy levels

INCREASE

BOOST

Your mood
Your brain power
Your positivity

Depression
Anxiety
Stress

REDUCE

Exercise is the most potent and yet underutilized antidepressant.

BILL PHILLIPS, AUTHOR AND ENTREPRENEUR

Exercise isn't a competition. It's win, win, WIN all the way.

Now, if you consider yourself a sporty type who already gets a lot of exercise from playing football, basketball or whatever, you could probably skip this section as no doubt you are ticking a lot of the right boxes already. Or stick around and feel smug, that's OK too.

But if, like me, gym or any sport is your most hated or feared lesson of all on your timetable – or at least very close to the top of that list – then do not despair as you are not alone – there will be others in your class who feel the same.

The good news is that there are plenty of fun ways to up your exercise. It is not uncommon for kids to come out of school hating sports, if physical activity isn't their thing. What follows are a few ideas to help you fight against that trend.

Remember, no one is expecting you to become the next Usain Bolt. Just move a little, then a little more and go from there.

Here are a few things you can do to get more exercise:

Go to the Park! – Suggest to your mates that you go to the park for a kick about or some sort of ball-related activity. You might only do said activity for ten minutes and then sit on the swings anyway but it's a good start.

Dance – Compile a playlist of songs that make you want to dance. Then when you hear it, get up and have a boogie. The beauty is, you can do this in the privacy of your own room and no-one will have to see. A great break for gamers!

Just Walk! – Whether it be walking to and from school, or meeting up with a friend for a chat and a stroll, studies have shown that walking just 20 minutes a day can stave off depression.

Run – Running is a good form of cardiovascular exercise (i.e. exercise that gets the heart pumping) that is quite simple to do. Consider downloading an app called Couch to 5k and make sure where you are running is safe. Maybe see if you can run with a friend or family member, but it is actually a really good solitary activity for the mind because it enables you to have time alone to process your thoughts, stresses and anxieties. Research carried out at King's College London found that running results in an increase in activity in an area of the brain called the anterior cortex, a key area for problem-solving and emotional resilience. That said, there are numerous running groups up and, erm, running around the country, and indeed world. One such organization that has gone global in recent years is parkrun – www.parkrun.com – which hold regular 5k running events in an increasing number of territories that the whole family can enjoy.

Try Starting Some Healthy Habits – Build little moments in your day when you can do short spurts of exercise. It could be a few push ups before you get dressed for school, or star jumps while your bread toasts – anything.

Keep it simple. In his book *Atomic Habits*, James Clear highlights the four laws of habits – pay particular attention to point 3:

"1. Make it obvious

2. Make it attractive

3. Make it easy

4. Make it satisfying."

Things to Remember:

Don't overdo it – if you haven't exercised very much in a long time, take any form of exercise step by step, e.g. a five-minute jog, interspersed with walking breaks, is probably more appropriate than attempting a three-mile run. If you are used to exercise, there is a tipping point when exercising too intensely will make you feel worse and more susceptible to injury. Even Olympic athletes know not to overtrain. Be kind to yourself!

Don't exercise too late in the day – it can make it hard for you to switch off and go to sleep.

Watch your diet – feed your body well so you are properly prepared to put it through its paces.

Give yourself a break – if, and hopefully when, you get to a stage where you are making exercise a regular part of your weekly routine, there will be times when you just don't feel like exercising, for whatever reason. Don't beat yourself up about this. Rest well and tell yourself that one day soon you can get back into your fabulous new way of keeping fit and healthy.

SLEEP WELL

Ah man, if you can get your sleeping right while you are teen, you will be winning at life, you really will. The World Health Organization (WHO) recommends getting eight to ten hours on a school night. So if you get up at 7 a.m., then that means going to bed between 9–10 p.m.

We have already seen that bad sleep is a symptom of various mental health conditions, in particular anxiety and stress, but we have yet to explore how good sleep can be a SUPERPOWER when it comes to keeping your mind in tip-top condition.

Yep, that's right... SUPERPOWER!

Look, before you scoff at the thought of sleep being a superpower, in 2014 Professor Matthew Walker, one of the world's leading experts on the subject of sleep, gave an amazing TedTalk called "Sleep Is Your Superpower". It's on YouTube, about 20 minutes long and well worth a watch.

To summarize, though, here are sleep's four main superpowers, i.e. some ways your mind and well-being will benefit the very next day from a good night's sleep**.

**A good night's sleep means eight hours of quality sleep where you go into a deep sleep, also known as REM sleep – REM as in "rapid eye movement" which is literally an indication of your brain processing information like an internal file transfer system – cool, eh?

SLEEP'S SUPERPOWER No. 1

Improves memory – if you have an exam or test, then double up your efforts to get a good night's sleep. If you have just been revising, the brain is more likely to compartmentalize your short-term memories into longer term ones.

SLEEP'S SUPERPOWER No. 2

Improves your ability to learn – that whole "it's a school night" thing is not just a myth. Having a good sleep means your mind will be sharper, more focused and be able to take in new information more easily.

SLEEP'S SUPERPOWER No. 3

Solves your problems – deep sleep also increases the opportunity for your brain to make fresh connections between different strands of information. Luis Fonsi first dreamed the melody which became the hook of his 2017 worldwide hit "Despacito" with Justin Bieber. Back in the 1960s, Paul McCartney woke up with the tune for a new song entitled "Scrambled Eggs" – wisely, he changed it to "Yesterday". While the Russian scientist Dmitri Mendeleev thanked his dreaming brain for helping him work out how to document the periodic table of elements, a task that had eluded him for years. That phrase "sleep on it" really is the basis for innovation.

SLEEP'S SUPERPOWER No. 4

Calms your emotions – we all have times where we might go to bed feeling ashamed of something that we said or did in the day but have you ever noticed that when you wake up, you remember how you felt and suddenly realize it doesn't feel quite as cringey or shameful. Well, guess what, that's deep sleep helping you to, as Professor Walker puts it, "calibrate your emotions". By this we mean deep sleep can take the sting out of those cringe moments and help us learn from the experience so next time we find ourselves in a similar situation, we are more likely to know what we should or shouldn't say or do and less likely to make a complete ass of ourselves, basically.

Now you probably can guess the sort of advice that is coming up... "Don't stay up too late!"

"Switch off the screens!" Well, yes, but it all depends on how you frame something, right – so why not take the Better Sleep Challenge...

TAKE THE BETTER SLEEP CHALLENGE

Bedtimes are for babies, right? Wrong! Sleep is a powerful "booster" to both our mental and physical health.

Good-quality sleep restores your mind, processing all the information that has accumulated in your head throughout the day so it is clear to take in more the next day. It's like pressing the restart button on your console.

Getting bad-quality sleep is like leaving it on with all manner of applications still running.

So why not take the Better Sleep Challenge and:

- **Switch off screens an hour before bed. The light keeps your brain awake.**
- **Read a book instead – or write in a journal/diary.**
- **Brush your teeth, get in your PJs BEFORE you feel tired.**
- **Avoid caffeine. No fizzy drinks. Instead, why not try a warm drink such as herbal tea or milky cocoa?**

All these will help prepare your mind for sleep.

And if that sounds like the most uninspiring challenge ever, don't despair... in your teens, your natural circadian rhythm – or body clock – shifts to a later time. You are able stay up later AND lie-in until midday at the weekend, guilt-free.*

*If your parents don't believe you, tell them to check out page 94 of the book Why We Sleep by Professor Matthew Walker who is Professor of Neuroscience and Psychology at the University of California.

TIP: A PLACE TO REST YOUR HEAD

Just use your bed for sleeping. Don't use it as a place to do your homework or even lie on to watch the television. Otherwise it will make it more difficult for your brain to associate the space with being the place where you sleep and you will struggle to nod off.

TIP: DON'T STRESS ABOUT IT

Don't stress about having a bad night's sleep, either during the night as you are drifting off or when you wake up. Do your best to get through the day by...

- Not panicking or stressing!
- Drinking lots of water
- Having a proper breakfast rather than a sugary cereal or snack
- Getting some fresh air or even going for a walk
- Taking a power nap, if possible
- Making sure you don't do too much – were you planning on meeting up in the park for a kickabout with your mates, or maybe doing lots of homework? – well, give yourself a break and don't put too much in your schedule, if you can
- Not panicking or stressing (I've said this again as it is extremely important...)

SELF-CARE, OR LOOKING AFTER YOURSELF PROPERLY

The accepted definition of self-care is "the practice of taking an active role in protecting one's own well-being and happiness" which is what this whole book is about. What I mean here, quite simply, is making sure you don't smell or feel icky.

You may think it's OK to go without having a bath or shower for a week and you just can't be bothered with all that preening malarkey but keeping yourself clean is a strong booster to improve your confidence, self-esteem and overall positivity.

If you have got an important project to finish for school, you will feel more ready and prepared to do your best if you feel clean and refreshed.

HYGIENE TIPS

You don't have to go out and buy lots of sweet-smelling soaps and shower gels. Just do the following...

- **Clean your teeth twice a day** – the power of fresh breath shouldn't be underestimated and having bad breath is associated with the development of social anxiety disorder.

- **Wash your hands regularly** – after going to the toilet, before you eat anything, etc.

- **Keep your nails short and dirt-free** – a weekly trim of your nails is a really good habit to get into.

- **Shower regularly** – like sleeping, showering can be a good activity to help you think through problems, plan your day or just switch your mind off for a few minutes. Same with having a bath, if you have time.

- **Remember to wash your hair with shampoo** – greasy hair looks horrible and doesn't feel pleasant at all.

- **Make sure you always have clean clothes** – put items of clothing in your wash basket and make sure your parents remember to wash them – and offer to help with the laundry from time to time as this will be a good life skill to learn.

BEING KIND TO YOURSELF

We should all be kind to others, right? But first and foremost we should always be kind to ourselves. Those moments in life where that voice in your head is mentally beating you up, telling you that you're useless or that you'll never achieve anything... you wouldn't ever speak to a friend that way, right? So remind yourself of that when you're next berating yourself in that way. Always be kind to yourself.

Talk to yourself as you would to someone you love.

BRENÉ BROWN, PROFESSOR

TAKING TIME OUT TO REFLECT AND BE CALM

Step away from the noise and the distractions of everyday life. Sit outside for ten minutes or switch off the Xbox and lie on your bed for a moment. Be like Ralph (although, granted, he'd have only had a Nintendo Wii in the nineteenth century.)

Doing this will really make you reflect on things that have happened in the day, whether they are good things, things that have made you laugh or the not so good things, in which case it will allow you the chance to put them in perspective. Were they really that bad? Do you really need to feel so sad in the grand scheme of things? Tomorrow's another day, a chance for you to feel happier or make up for anything that may have gone wrong. At this point, it is worth suggesting that not only should you be like Ralph but you should also be like Ashton...

> # Nothing can bring you peace but yourself.
>
> ### RALPH WALDO EMERSON, NINETEENTH-CENTURY PHILOSOPHER

Take a long pause...
breathe and know
that things are
happening for
you, not to you.

ASHTON KUTCHER, ACTOR

PRACTISE SOME MINDFULNESS AKA A GOOD WAY TO LOOK AFTER YOUR MIND

The dictionary definition of mindfulness is:

> A mental state achieved by focusing one's awareness on the present moment, while calmly acknowledging and accepting one's feelings, thoughts, and bodily sensations; used as a therapeutic technique.

In other words, it is a technique that, with practice, trains you to focus your mind on one particular sense at a time, with the benefit that this will completely detract from any stress or anxiety you are going through. Those negative emotions should literally feel as though they have melted away because you shouldn't be thinking about them, even if it is just for a few moments.

Think of mindfulness as the key to looking after your own mental health – and it needn't take up too much of your time. Presenting...

FIVE MINDFULNESS METHODS YOU CAN DO IN FIVE MINUTES:

Dance – don't just listen to your favourite song while you're playing on your PlayStation. Close your bedroom door, turn on the song and dance. Close your eyes and really focus on the song. It really will help your mind move away from all the things whirring inside of it.

Do a Puzzle – a crossword, word search, spot the difference, anything. So long as it is taxing enough to allow your mind to focus on it and forget everything else – and, ideally, you are not doing it on a screen but in a puzzle book or newspaper.

Go Outside – walk around and let your mind go blank by focusing on nature around you. Look closely at the flowers, listen to the insects and even the rustling of small animals. It will really clear your head.

Have a Bath – always good from a hygiene point of view, of course, but immersing yourself in a hot bath unleashes all manner of sensations on your body and is a treat for four of your five senses (maybe not taste!).

Colour in – you don't have to be a great artist to sit down for a few minutes and colour in a picture. The act of colouring requires enough concentration to keep your mind focused on the task in hand and not worrying about anything else.

LEARN TO GROW IN CONFIDENCE

Confidence is a feeling of self-assurance that arises from an appreciation of your own qualities and abilities. Having a good level of confidence can do wonders for your mental health. If it is something you feel like you don't have, then you can grow it through various methods we have already discussed, including positive thinking and being kind to yourself.

Often we associate confidence with excelling in a certain activity or being able to stand out from the crowd in some way. All well and good of course, but it is possible to be quietly confident too. Here are three tips inspired by life strategist Stefan James:

Do not fear silence. Listening is a far more powerful tool than speaking.

Challenge yourself to grow, without bragging to your mates about what you are going to do. The latter opens you up to peer pressure and doesn't allow you to make mistakes on your own terms.

Do not seek the limelight. Instead praise others and inspire them to become the best version of themselves. Hopefully you can learn to talk to yourself in a similar way.

BE A FEMINIST

If you are reading this book, in all likelihood you were assigned male at birth (i.e. the medical staff said, "it's a boy") and, biologically, you have been a boy all your life so far. Which means no matter what you do, you will never, ever know what it is like to be a girl.

Being a teenage boy can be tough but being a teenage girl is TOUGHER, for reasons I won't go into here but, suffice to say, women continue to fight for equality in many different ways and girls still suffer from sexism and discrimination in school, as well as when they get older.

Of course, things have come a long way in fighting against the inequality and discrimination and society is changing. The point I am making here is that there are things you can do to help this change.

Look closely, and sexism is most likely still present in your school. Listen to some of the derogatory language your peers use when talking about, and even to, girls. Don't contribute to it. Find a way to challenge it. Real friends will listen to you, the others aren't worth hanging out with. Never feel that you have to use this language or behave in a certain way toward women to fit in because, a) it is fundamentally wrong, and b) it won't come to any good, it just won't.

What's this got to do with your mental health? Well, you'll be doing the right thing and doing the right thing is a great "booster" to your confidence and self-esteem, knowing others will see you in this light. Being mindful and kind toward people, no matter who they are, is a wonderful feeling to carry with you and a brilliant example to set with everyone else.

SEXUALITY

This is a very important taboo for us to discuss when it comes to your mental health. If you are sure you like girls, then you have things relatively easy, well aside from all the complications brought on by fancying someone who doesn't fancy you back, awkward exchanges during school breaks, the pain of splitting up with someone, the list goes on.

But it might not be quite as straightforward as that for you. Your teenage years are a time when, sooner or later, you will discover your sexuality. While for some, that involves realizing the type of girls you like, for others it is time when you might discover you like boys and are gay, or you like boys and girls and are bisexual. You could also be confused as to your gender and you should have the freedom to ask questions and seek support.

Your sexual identity might be something that you have felt sure of for some time, but only in your teenage years might it feel like something you can explore. But it's also worth saying that you might not work it out fully until you're in your 20s – and that's OK!

Now hopefully you have a good support network in your family and circle of friends where you can maybe discuss these feelings and, if you feel like it, "come out" to the people you love and who love you unconditionally in return. Your sexuality, whatever it may be, is something to be celebrated and you should never ever feel ashamed.

Unfortunately, not everyone has a support network as strong as that, specifically where their family is concerned. The thought of going to their parents and other family members and saying "I'm gay", "I'm bisexual" or "non-binary", fills some kids with dread, like they are going to be disowned, hated or even kicked out of the house, even though we are well into the twenty-first century and most people are supportive of the LGBTQIA+ community.

It is worth pointing out that this community is a big one and it is likely you will know someone your age going through a similar battle with who they are. It is so important to not try to escape who you are but rather celebrate it.

This is easier said than done for some people and there are organizations and support groups, no doubt in your area, who can help (check out the suggestions on page 153 too). So do make contact with them, because not dealing with your feelings and pretending to be someone who you are not will greatly impact your mental health for years to come.

Remember, as I said at the start of this book, and have repeated a few times during it: you are brilliant.

Chapter 6

HOW TO LOOK OUT FOR OTHERS

So how do you feel now that you have learned some ways to look after your own mental health?

Well-informed?
Empowered?
Bored?

OK, who said bored? That's just rude.

Hopefully, though, you will have chosen one or both of the first two. Let's focus now on that second one: empowered. Because you will find that it is empowering to know that you have those "boosters" in your armoury, like eating more healthily and sleeping well that will strengthen you if ever you need to go into battle with a mental health issue. In the meantime, they will keep your mind in a good place.

The knock-on effect is that you will feel more able to do well at school, excel at a hobby or chosen sport, keep up meaningful relationships with friends that you know are good for you to hang out with.

THAT'S what it means to feel empowered.

So while you are in a good place, what about challenging this feeling of empowerment and paying it forward? You might not think that there is anyone in your life at the moment who is going through mental health issues of their own. In all likelihood, you will be wrong.

In this chapter we will look at the signs to pick up on that a friend or family member might be struggling with a mental health issue, but perhaps they do not feel they can open up about their difficulties.

And that's where YOU may be able to help.

In this chapter we ask: how should you broach the subject with them? And when should you back off and find another way to help? What should you do if it's clear the person involved requires the support of a professional? Of course, sometimes a friend might approach you with their mental health problem. We look at how to handle that situation. Finally, we will list scenarios that might not make you think someone has a problem at all but there may well be indicators that said person is having mental health issues of their own – e.g. if someone is being annoying or proving difficult to get along with. It is easy to dismiss them and not give them the time of day, but perhaps they are going through something such as anxiety or grief that is making them behave that way.

YOU DON'T HAVE TO BE A MENTAL HEALTH SUPERMAN

Ultimately, you are a kid and you cannot be expected to shoulder the responsibility of having to deal with another person's mental health issue, whoever that person might be. If it is a close relative who needs help, speak to another (grown-up) close relative who can share the burden and worry that often comes with being a confidant of someone suffering from poor mental health.

In this chapter you will learn how to:

- **be aware of someone's difficulties**
- **get them to open up if possible**
- **listen to what they've been going through and how they are feeling**
- **signpost them toward the right organization or place that can lead them to being able to manage their mental health condition**

It would be irresponsible for any book to get you to do any more than this for someone, certainly on your own. Keep listening, keep talking, keep signposting but don't let the buck stop with you, because that's not just unfair on you but it is unfair for the person who needs help.

SIGNS THAT SOMEONE IS SUFFERING FROM A MENTAL HEALTH ISSUE

So do you think you would be able to spot if a friend or family member is struggling with their mental health? There are a number of signs to look for, many of which we have seen as symptoms in previous chapters. They are:

- **Change of eating habits** – if they seem to be eating more or less, both can indicate an issue. Stress might cause someone to eat more, anxiety might lead someone to eat less. Eating less and losing a lot of weight in a short time could, of course, be a sign of an eating disorder.

- **Mood swings** – moods can shift in a number of ways. If someone is usually cheery and upbeat but has increasingly frequent occasions of being quiet and withdrawn, this is a strong indicator of depression. If they go the opposite way and have unusual moments of hyperactivity followed by low moments, this suggests it could be bipolar disorder. Meanwhile, if someone seems angrier than usual, shouting at people or even just at the world around them, this is likely to be an indication of stress or something more deeprooted, such as their frustrations regarding a situation in their personal life that they have been unable to change for a long time – maybe a parent has left the family home or they are below the poverty line and go without things that you might take for granted. These reasons should never be an excuse for their bad behaviour but may well be an explanation.

- **Low self-esteem** – is the person always putting themselves down? Again, this could point to depression and if they have always had low self-esteem, the depression could be quite deep rooted.

- **Withdrawing from people and things they love** – if a friend or family member isn't being as social as they usually are, staying in their room a lot or isolating themselves from their friends in school, the very least you can do is ask why they think they might be behaving like that.

- **Forgetfulness/not sleeping properly/lacking in energy** – all of these point toward their mind being overloaded with stress, anxiety or some other mental health condition. It is difficult for anyone to pinpoint at this stage but definitely a good indicator that something is bothering them. So, again, ask.

- **Behaving out of character** – of course, this covers all the above points but there might be something specific about your friend or family member that you noticed has changed, such as your friend's ability to always do well in school tests. Or if a parent is drinking more than usual. These are all good triggers to get you to ask what's wrong and see if they need help.

MENTAL HEALTH ICEBREAKERS

What do you say to someone who you suspect is suffering from a mental health issue? Here are the top five icebreakers, in no particular order, that will keep this very important conversation going:

- **"Let's go somewhere quiet to talk"** – the perfect way to eliminate the pressure of feeling someone else will be listening; it might also involve getting away from another person who might actually be the root of the problem, e.g. a nasty teacher or inconsiderate relative.

- **"Do you want to talk about it?"** – this helps them feel in control of the situation and remember if they say no, you can ask them again another time.

- **"How are you coping?"** – this gives the person the opportunity to review what they have been doing so far to manage their mental health condition.

- **"Shall I speak or listen?"** – the person might just want to sound off and keep talking but at appropriate pauses in the conversation, you can offer up your opinion or perspective.

- **"What can I do to help?"** – you can't resolve their issue but there might be certain things you can do for them, from hanging out with them for a while, to fixing them a snack – little gestures can go a long way.

TIP: WHAT TO DO IF A FRIEND OPENS UP TO YOU

Similar rules apply to the mental health icebreakers and can be summarized quite succinctly:

- LISTEN – if they're talking, let them talk and allow them to pause for a few moments – you don't have to say anything until you truly sense they are waiting to hear something from you

- REASSURE – e.g. "you've done the right thing by opening up" and "I'm always here if you need a chat".

- VALIDATE – i.e. say things like, "what you are going through is tough, no wonder you feel like that".

- HELP – again the smallest gesture like a hug will help the person know you care.

- SIGNPOST – point them in the direction of their doctor, or an organization that will provide further, and maybe ongoing, support.

TIP: HOW TO GET A FRIEND TO OPEN UP TO YOU

Here are four simple steps to follow if you suspect your friend might be affected by a mental health issue.

1   Check in – just by hanging out with a friend and asking questions such as "how are you?" or "how are things at school?" or "how are things at home?" will give them a chance to get something off their chest. Mention anything that you might already know about what could be affecting them, such as a recent bereavement, because this may lead them into talking more about how this particular event or situation is making them feel.

2   Show you care by listening – we already know the importance of listening but also make sure you are paying attention to what they are saying. All you need to say is that you are there for them and keep on listening to them. You are helping them feel heard, appreciated and valued.

3   Offer support, not advice. **Unless you are a mental health professional (unlikely), you are not there to provide a solution. The best thing you can ask is: "what can I do to help?" This gives the person a feeling of control, which is vital when you are used to being overwhelmed by a mental health condition. They might not ask for very much help from you but the fact that they do means they are more likely to ask and accept help when they are sitting in front of a mental health professional.**

4   Assure them you're there for the long term – **if you can guide them toward getting further support, then great – but if not, just let them know you will be there to listen to them share their feelings any time they feel like it.**

TIP: WHAT IF YOUR FRIEND DOESN'T WANT TO TALK?

Well, don't push it as you are likely to cause an argument and threaten your friendship, which would mean you might never be able to help them. So just say, "well, if you ever want to talk, I'm here," and step away. Give them space. They know they have the option to come to you. And then, DON'T GIVE UP ON THEM. Keep an eye out for them and, from time to time, when it feels comfortable, ask how they are doing and see if they are ready to open up. Or drop them a text and give them the option to respond when they are truly ready. You never know, they may already have sought help for themselves, perhaps even because you attempted to reach out to them before. So don't lose heart or ever feel bad if your efforts to show support are rebuffed. It doesn't mean they won't make a difference.

TIP: HORRIBLE/MEAN/RUDE PEOPLE AND WHAT MIGHT BE BOTHERING THEM

Now that you have some appreciation of the effects a mental health condition can have on someone, it may make you think twice when you encounter someone who is being horrible, rude or mean.

Although poor mental health shouldn't excuse someone's behaviour completely, it could at least explain it and, even if you can never be sure that it is the reason for such behaviour, leave you feeling able to rise above it.

Who am I referring to? Well, here are three examples:

- **School bullies** – bullies can crop up anywhere but school is the most likely place you will encounter them. Of course they shouldn't behave in the appalling way that they do but it is worth stopping for a moment to consider what life might be like for them at home and maybe there is some trauma that has happened to them that makes them feel the need to be horrible to others. Flag it with a trusted adult in a position to offer support to them.

- **Angry parents** – what could be worrying them or stressing them out that you don't know about? You might have something of an insight of what the problem might be but you won't know the full details. The best thing to do is to give them a hug in their calmer moments and give them space during the less calm ones – but reach out to a teacher if you ever feel scared or threatened at home.

- **Mean teachers** – not that there is anything you could do to help them but there is almost always a reason, not an excuse, for someone's meanness. It could be low self-esteem driving a need to feel powerful or some traumatic event from their past where they have been belittled. No teacher should ever take this out on their pupil but there are a handful that do and so it is very important to emphasize that it's not you, it's them!

There is no need to suffer silently and there is no shame in seeking help.

CATHERINE ZETA JONES, ACTRESS

Chapter 7

WHERE TO GET HELP (AND HOW TO GET HELP)

If you have started this chapter with the intention of actually seeking further help, can I just take this moment to say...

What you are about to do is BRILLIANT and BRAVE and without any doubt, it's going to help you get your mental health back on track.

We have already covered starting a conversation about your own mental health with people you know, and also how to broach the topic when you think a friend or relative is going through a bad time but where can YOU go for further help?

In this chapter, we will list a variety of charities and organizations that you can contact for help, advice and support. Some offer support for mental health issues in general whilst others focus on specific issues such as depression.

Now if the thought of having to speak to a stranger about something so sensitive and personal fills you with dread, you will be pleased to know that many of these organizations have alternatives to the old-fashioned phone lines. You can arrange to speak to a trained volunteer via an online web chat, while some even allow you to text.

We begin with a general list on page 147 and then feature some more specialized organizations from page 151 onwards. These are broken down in the categories of the mental health conditions that they focus on, listed in alphabetical order.

There are still so many people suffering in silence. And there's still this stigma attached to mental health which we've got to completely obliterate.

PRINCE WILLIAM, DUKE OF CAMBRIDGE

TIP: DO WHATEVER MAKES YOU FEEL MOST COMFORTABLE

Texting might be an attractive option at first but it also might begin to feel a little detached from the person you are communicating with. So ask if you can switch. Ditto if you are on the phone and suddenly feel you would prefer talking over email or text. Don't just hang up. Tell the person on the line and they will doubtless do their best to help.

BUT I STILL DON'T WANT TO SEEK HELP!

If you're still not sure about opening up to someone you might not know, like a doctor or a charity volunteer, let's look at the main reasons why you might not want to seek help.

Reason 1: I feel ashamed

The big one has to be a feeling of shame. You're embarrassed, right? By saying out loud the words: "I need help", it feels like you're owning up to a weakness. I get it.

But can we just get back to the whole physical health vs mental health thing. You'd go and seek professional help if you broke your leg, wouldn't you? There'd be no need for embarrassment or shame in getting a cast put on that leg.

It is exactly the same as seeking help for your mental health. There are many doctors and health professionals who have been trained in mental health and have heard similar symptoms in other people your age, so they will know what the best thing to help you feel better will be.

Remember: your teenage years are a rollercoaster of emotions and feeling big feelings is a normal and healthy part of growing up.

Reason 2: Will anyone believe me?

If you can slowly speak about the way you have been feeling and the occasions where your mental health has been affected, then the doctor or health professional will just know that you are not making it up.

Just because you are talking about a part of yourself that cannot be seen or easily examined doesn't mean it isn't real. Mental health issues aren't in your imagination – they are a real thing.

Reason 3: Do my friends or family have to know?

And what will your mates think? Or even your brother or sister? Well, they don't need to know. Like with your physical health, doctors and health professionals must deal with your issue in complete confidence. It may surprise you to learn this but they won't even speak to your parents if you don't want them to – though, they might advise that you share what you are going through with them. The choice is yours.

A GUIDE TO SEEKING COUNSELLING OR THERAPY THROUGH YOUR DOCTOR OR SCHOOL

Doctor! Referrals! Counselling! Therapy! It all can sound so scary! But really, it isn't. To hopefully put you at ease, here is a guide to the kind of process you can expect.

1   At the initial appointment with your doctor, they will talk to you about your mental health and discuss what options are available to you. You don't actually have to be diagnosed with a specific mental health condition to have counselling.

2   If you and your doctor are in agreement as to the next course of action, they will organize a referral. In the UK, this will likely mean referring you to the Child and Adolescent Mental Health Services (CAMHS). In the US, you could well be directed to the Substance Abuse and Mental Health Services Administration (SAMHSA). There might be a waiting list and if so, your doctor may well suggest other avenues of support to carry you through in the meantime.

3   Counselling involves talking about your thoughts, feelings and experiences to help you work out what is going on in your life.

It can help you find ways of coping when things are difficult. Counselling is usually short term for a specific problem that you might be struggling with right now – for example, if you have recently lost a loved one, you will probably be referred to a grief counsellor.

4   Therapy is also a talking treatment but the main difference is that it is more long term, where you are struggling for a while and it is impacting your life but you can't figure out why. Therapy offers a deeper dive over a longer period of time so you can figure out what is causing you to struggle and find solutions to overcome the problems.

5   Your first session with your counsellor or therapist will involve them discussing what you should expect from the sessions, which will usually be weekly. They will also explain practical things like how long the course of sessions might last and what to do if you can't attend one week. Don't be afraid to ask whatever questions occur to you. There will also be time to start talking about the reason why you are there.

6   The subsequent sessions will involve more talking. Again, be honest – and if there is anything you feel too uncomfortable speaking about, tell your counsellor or therapist. It might be something you can come back to later.

7   How long will the course last? This will have been mentioned in your first session but it is something that is fluid and you can ask your counsellor or therapist about having more sessions. They might be able to speak to your doctor for you. Alternatively, you can return to your doctor and request more sessions, or a different counsellor if you think it hasn't worked for you so far.

TIP: SEE YOUR DOCTOR ONLINE

Contacting your doctor in the first place may be a daunting prospect but hopefully you have a parent or guardian who can help you arrange an appointment, without needing to know exactly why.

Many surgeries offer telephone advice. You can call the surgery, leave your number and a GP will phone you back. Some surgeries may even be able to organize a Zoom call.

If this sounds too daunting, most surgeries connect to the NHS's eConsult service (www.econsult.net/nhs-patients) where you can find more information on an array of conditions, including mental health ones.

You can then opt to answer a series of questions relating to the condition and your experiences and have your GP get back in touch with you but this part of the service is only available if you are over 18. So you will need a parent to act on your behalf if you do want a call back from the surgery. If up until now you've felt uncomfortable talking to your parents about your issue, the eConsult website and service might be a good icebreaker to open the conversation.

GENERAL MENTAL HEALTH SUPPORT

If you're looking for general support for your mental health, then these are the organizations to approach. They may very well guide you to another organization that is listed in this chapter.

Childline

Who Are They? A private and confidential helpline for young people where you can talk about anything, including mental health.

Special features: Email a trained counsellor by registering and sending a message from your "locker". You can also play games and draw pictures online to show how you are feeling and, if signed up, you can send them to a trained counsellor.

Phone: 0800 1111

Web chat: Yes

Website: www.childline.org.uk

In the US, call the Childhelp National Child Abuse Hotline 24/7 on (1-800) 4-A-Child or (1-800) 422-4453

Crisis Text Line

Who Are They? Crisis Text Line provides free, 24/7, high-quality text-based mental health support and crisis intervention by empowering a community of trained volunteers to support people in their moments of need.

UK: Text 85258
Ireland: Text 50808
US or Canada: Text 741741

Kooth

Who Are They? A digital mental health community for young adults.

Special features: Speak to the friendly and experienced Kooth team about anything on your mind or start a conversation with members of the community. Free, safe and anonymous support. You can also track your feelings using a private, online daily journal.

Website: www.kooth.com

National Alliance On Mental Illness (NAMI) (US)

Who Are They? NAMI provides advocacy, education, support and public awareness so that all individuals and families affected by mental illness can build better lives.

Phone: 1-800-950-NAMI (6264)
Email: info@nami.org
Website: www.nami.org

On My Mind

Who Are They? A space for empowering young people to make informed choices about their mental health and well-being.

Special features: Hosts the AFC Crisis Messenger Service where anyone who is feeling overwhelmed and is struggling to cope can text trained volunteers for support. There is also a wide variety of resources curated and produced by young people, including understanding referrals, dealing with loss and bereavement and helping someone else.

Text: AFC to 85258 to receive crisis help from a trained volunteer.

Website: www.annafreud.org/on-my-mind

Samaritans

Who Are They? An organization that is there to listen to you, whatever you are going though.

Phone: 116 123

Email: jo@samaritans.org

Website: www.samaritans.org

Substance Abuse And Mental Health Services Administration (SAMHSA) (US)

Who Are They? A national helpline that is free and confidential, providing support for individuals facing mental and/or substance use disorders and their families.

Helpline: 1-800-6620-HELP (4357)

Website: www.samhsa.gov/find-help

Supportline

Who Are They? A charity providing a confidential helpline for anyone in need of emotional support for any issue, whatever their age.
Phone: 01708 765200
Email: info@supportline.org.uk
Website: www.supportline.org.uk

Teen Line (US)

Who Are They? Provides support, resources and hope to young people through a hotline of trained teen counsellors and outreach programmes that destigmatize and normalize mental health.
Phone: 800-852-8336
Text: Text TEEN to 839863
Email: via their website teenline.org/email-us
Website: www.teenline.org

Young Minds

Who Are They? A leading charity in the UK that is working toward making sure young people have access to all the mental health support they need. There are lots of in-depth resources on their website.
Special features: A text line staffed by trained volunteers who are supported by experienced clinical supervisors.
Text: YM to 85258
Website: www.youngminds.org.uk

SPECIALIZED SUPPORT

Anxiety:

Anxiety UK

Who Are They? A charity formed in 1970 to help those affected by anxiety, stress and anxiety-related depression.

Special features: Support from trained staff, many of whom have experience of the isolation, misery and distress that anxiety can cause.

Phone: 03444 775 774
Text: 07537 416905
Email: support@anxietyuk.org.uk
Website: www.anxietyuk.org.uk

Bereavement:

Hope Again

Who Are They? This is the youth website of Cruse Bereavement Care, offering support and advice for young people who have lost a loved one.

Special Features: If someone you know has died, you can send a private email to a trained volunteer or you can call the Cruse helpline directly.

Email: hopeagain@cruse.org.uk
Phone: 0808 808 1677
Website: www.hopeagain.org.uk

Eating Disorders:

BEAT

Who Are They? A charity who offer support and information for people of all ages about eating disorders, no matter whether you suspect you have a problem, are awaiting treatment or have come through your condition.

Phone: 0808 801 0711

Email: fyp@beateatingdisorders.org.uk

Web chat: Yes

Website: www.beateatingdisorders.org.uk

National Eating Disorders Association Hotline (US)

Who Are They? A hotline providing support, referrals, information and guidance about treatment options for either you or a loved one.

Phone: 1-800-931-2237

Text: Text NEDA to 741741

Website: www.nationaleatingdisorders.org

Hearing Voices:

Voice Collective

Who Are They? An organization providing support for people under 25 who hear voices, have visions or other unusual sensory experiences or beliefs. Lots of helpful resources, including an online support forum. You have to register to use the forum and it is closely moderated.

Website: www.voicecollective.co.uk

OCD:

OCD Youth

Who Are They? A youth-led initiative for young people run by volunteers under 25 who have all had experiences with obsessive-compulsive disorder (OCD). It aims to raise awareness of and increase access to support for the condition.

Email: youthhelpline@ocdaction.org.uk

Website: www.ocdaction.org

Panic Attacks:

No Panic

Who Are They? A charity offering support for people who suffer from panic attacks, as well as OCD, phobias and anxiety. The listed number is a specific helpline for young people.

Phone: 0330 606 1174

Website: www.nopanic.org.uk

Sexuality and Gender:

Mermaids

Who are they? A safe place for transgender, non-binary and gender-diverse young people to find support and help one another. Providing assistance and advice for people under 20, the organization was originally set up by concerned parents in 1995 to keep their children safe and happy while giving them the freedom and confidence to explore their gender identity free from fear, isolation and discrimination.

Special features: Lots of online resources and connections to local community groups.
Phone: 0808 801 0400
Email: info@mermaidsuk.org.uk
Text: Mermaids to 85258
Web Chat: Yes (for people under 25)
Website: www.mermaidsuk.org.uk

Mindline Trans+

Who are they? An emotional and mental health support helpline for anyone identifying as transgender, non-binary, genderfluid, etc. Totally confidential – they won't even ask for your name. Monday, Wednesday and Friday evenings 8 p.m.–midnight only.
Phone: 0300 330 5468
Website: www.mindlinetrans.org.uk

Mindout

Who are they? A mental health service for the LGBTQ+ community run by members within it who have experienced mental health issues.
Phone: 01273 234 839
Email: info@mindout.org.uk
Web chat: Yes
Website: www.mindout.org.uk

The Proud Trust

Who are they? An organization providing resources for LGBTQ+ young people.

Phone: 0161 660 3347
Web chat: Yes (Tuesday and Thursday afternoons only)
Website: www.theproudtrust.org

Stonewall

Who are they? An organization that stands for LGBQT+ people everywhere in the hope they can be free to be who they are and live life to the full.
Switchboard LGBT: https://switchboard.lgbt/
Email: info@stonewall.org.uk
Website: www.stonewall.org.uk

Having suicidal thoughts? Then visit one of these websites or call one of the helpline numbers as soon as you can.

Papyrus Hopeline UK

Phone: 0800 068 4141
Text: 07860 039967
www.papyrus-uk.org

Samaritans

Phone: UK – 116 123
US – (1-800) 273-TALK

National Suicide Prevention Line (US)

Phone: 800-273-TALK (8255)

TIP: BE PREPARED!

Having made the decision to reach out to someone for help, whether that be a doctor, a counsellor through school or one of the organizations we've included, it is a good idea to maximize your use of time when speaking to them.

- Write down some notes, or just a few trigger words, covering everything you want to share and say. Other things may occur to you during the conversation but any notes will give you a starting point and help you to avoid freezing up mid-session.
- Be honest! Everything you share will be confidential. Don't feel that you have to hide anything – it will feel better to get it out in the open to someone. Above all, don't tell your doctor or counsellor what you think they want to hear!
- Find out as many alternative courses of action as possible. You might be set on getting some medication from your doctor but be open-minded enough to ask for information on alternative therapies that might be suitable and how beneficial they will be in comparison. Again, have a list of questions and concerns prepared.
- If you are not satisfied with how the appointment has gone, you can always seek a second opinion from another professional, whether that means asking your doctor to refer you to a different counsellor or speaking to a different organization altogether.

CONCLUSION

So here we are, at the end of the book, except in many respects it is only the beginning.

Hopefully I've brought you lots of good advice about how best to look after your mental health and maybe you will even keep it handy for when you feel you need a few prompts to keep your well-being up there in the "highest scorers" league.

But one last thought... remember, nobody is perfect. Yeah, yeah, I know I just said "you are brilliant" at the end of the last chapter but brilliance is different from perfection. We are always going to have off days where we don't do the best for ourselves.

Indeed looking back at my diary from when I was 14, I spent the vast majority of my summer holiday that year in my room making magazines and comics and watching old episodes of a show called *Happy Days* and the odd Laurel and Hardy film. I made no mention of seeing any friends or even going outside very much. On the one hand, 14-year-old me could have done with this book to get me out in the fresh air and interacting with people. On the other hand, I didn't turn out too bad.

What I am trying to say is: don't let this book, or anything, put unnecessary pressure on you. Do what you can but don't sweat what you can't, OK?

And if ever you need a nudge in the right direction, well, get talking...

ABOUT THE AUTHOR

Adam Carpenter is a writer and editor who currently works in Digital Safety and Community for a global kidtech company. He lives in West Cornwall, United Kingdom, with his wife and two children. This is his second book.